Lincoln Painted by Charles M. Shean

Abraham Lincoln
An Illustrated Biography
in Postcards

James D. Ristine

4880 Lower Valley Road, Atglen, PA 19310

Published by Schiffer Publishing Ltd.
4880 Lower Valley Road
Atglen, PA 19310
Phone: (610) 593-1777; Fax: (610) 593-2002
E-mail: Info@schifferbooks.com

For the largest selection of fine reference books on this and related subjects,
please visit our web site at **www.schifferbooks.com**
We are always looking for people to write books on new and related subjects. If you have an idea for a book please contact us at the above address.

This book may be purchased from the publisher.
Include $3.95 for shipping.
Please try your bookstore first.
You may write for a free catalog.

In Europe, Schiffer books are distributed by
Bushwood Books

Other Schiffer Books on Related Subjects

Collecting Lincoln, Stuart Schneider., ISBN: 0-7643-0270-1, hard cover, $69.95

Schiffer Books are available at special discounts for bulk purchases for sales promotions or pre-
miums. Special editions, including personalized covers, corporate imprints, and excerpts can
be created in large quantities for special needs. For more information contact the publisher:

Designed by Ro Shillingford
Type set in Zurich BT

ISBN: 978-0-7643-2857-2
Printed in China

Contents

Introduction   5
A Brief Guide to the History of Postcards   7
Chapter 1: Humble Beginnings (1809-1830)   10
Chapter 2: Road to the White House (1831–1860)   18
Chapter 3: The Presidency & the Civil War (1861-1865)   36
Chapter 4: Assassination & the Journey Home (1865)   55
Chapter 5: Portraits & Photographs   75
Chapter 6: His Lasting Words   97
Chapter 7: Monuments and Memorials   113
Bibliography   144

© 1909, R. Sander, New York, NY [$12-15]

Acknowledgments

I was fortunate to have grown up in a home in which there were a number of books on the life of Abraham Lincoln. My parents nurtured in me a great interest in American history and for this I am eternally grateful. Many thanks also go out to my sister Barbara, who passed on to me a shoe box full of old postcards that had belonged to our grandfather. Little did she know that this would motivate me to begin collecting antique postcards and ultimately lead to the writing of this book. I am deeply appreciative of my wife Deborah who helped enormously in the editing and proofreading of my work. Also instrumental in the production of this book was my editor Tina Skinner at Schiffer Publishing. She guided me through the process of producing this book and making it a reality. Thanks also to Debra Gust, and those at Lake County (IL) Discovery Museum, Curt Teich Postcard Archives, for granting me permission to use postcard images published by the Curt Teich Company.

Lastly, acknowledgment is given to the many historians and authors who have written about the life of this great man. And much gratitude to all those photographers and publishers of the many postcards that have helped document the life of Abraham Lincoln.

c. 1906, Publisher unknown [$6-8]

c. 1910, Raphael Tuck & Sons, London, England [$20-22]

c. 1906, Publisher unknown [$6-8]

1908, M.T. Sheahan, Boston, MA [$4-6]

Introduction

There is no individual in American History who has been written about more than Abraham Lincoln. Thousands of books, innumerable magazine and newspaper articles, and countless television and movie productions have dealt with the life of this great man. Just hearing his name or seeing it in print brings images and conceptions of the man to mind.

He was a man who came from the simplest of beginnings to become an American icon. During his lifetime he was a farmer, rail splitter, store clerk, soldier, surveyor, lawyer, and politician. Largely self educated, he demonstrated that with hard work and perseverance a person could achieve great things. As William Herndon, one of his law partners, said of him, "his ambition was a little engine that knew no rest."

As our 16th President, he would guide our country during the time of its greatest turmoil, the Civil War. Part of his legacy is that his actions and decisions helped hold our nation together and, ultimately, he was able to abolish the institution of slavery. Assassinated early in his second term of office he never lived to see his deam of a reunited nation realized.

The purpose of this book is to provide a concise and chronological telling of the major events and happenings that shaped the life of this remarkable individual, and, in so doing, to demonstrate how his life and achievements influenced and shaped the history and culture of our nation.

What sets this book apart from so many others is that it illustrates the life of Abraham Lincoln through the use of postcard images. Many thousands of different postcards have been published over the years pertaining in some way to this great man. These have helped to document his image, his accomplishments, the places and events that were important in his life, his words, and the many monuments and memorials erected in his honor. This book utilizes a representative sampling of such postcards. For the benefit of collectors of Lincoln-related materials and those postcard collectors interested in this particular topic, a price guide with publisher information have been provided.

It is the author's hope that the reader will not only find the text interesting and informative, but will also gain an appreciation for the life and significant achievements of Abraham Lincoln.

c. 1910, R. Sander, New York, NY [$4-6]

ABRAHAM LINCOLN: born in Kentucky, 1809; assassinated at Washington, 1865; admitted to bar in Illinois, 1836; captain in Black Hawk war, 1832; member of Congress, 1847-49; famous debate on slavery with Stephen A. Douglas in 1848; elected president in 1860 by electoral vote of 180 against 123; his election was the signal for the beginning of the secession movement; re-elected president in 1864.

© 1908, R.M. Donaldson [$15-20]

c. 1909, Publisher unknown [$6-8]

© 1909, P. Sander, New York, NY [$8-12]

c. 1909, Paul Finkenroth, Berlin, Germany [$12-15]

A Brief Guide to the
History of Postcards

PIONEER ERA (1893-1898)
It is generally believed that the first picture postcards in the United States were sold at the Columbian Exposition in Chicago in May, 1893. The backs of these cards were undivided and often printed with the words "Souvenir Card" or "Mail Card." Writing was not permitted on the address side of the card. Studies have shown that some advertising postcards existed prior to 1893.

PRIVATE MAILING CARD ERA (1898-1901)
Cards from this era are identified by the printed inscription "Private Mailing Card, Authorized by Act of Congress on May 19, 1898." Correspondence was still not allowed on the back of the card.

UNDIVIDED BACK ERA (1901-1907)
The words "Post Card" are printed on the back of the card and the cards have an undivided back. Only the address of the recipient is permitted on the back, resulting in many cards having a message written on the picture side of the card.

DIVIDED BACK ERA (1907-1915)
The back is divided on these cards, allowing for both the address and message to appear on the same side. The front side of the card was filled with the pictorial image. This is the time period sometimes referred to as the "Golden Age of Postcards," as postcards became a worldwide collecting craze. United States postal records indicate that in the fiscal year 1908 some 677,777,798 postcards were mailed!

WHITE BORDER ERA (1915-1930)
Due to World War I, postcards, which had primarily been printed in Germany, began to be printed in this country. These cards are easy to identify because of the white border around the image on front of the card.

LINEN ERA (1930-1945)
Cards from this era are printed on paper with a high rag content, creating a linen-like appearance and feel to the card.

MODERN CHROME ERA (1945-present)
These Photochrome cards, or "Chromes" as they are commonly called, utilize printing techniques, which allow for high photographic quality and bright colors.

Price Guide
The price guide in this book is based on the author's personal experience in purchasing postcards for his own collection, as well as prices seen in dealer stock at postcard shows, antique markets, and on the Internet. Values to cards are not set in stone and can vary greatly in some instances, with condition being a major factor. This is to be used as a guideline only. Remember that a card's true value is only what you are willing to pay for it. Dates of publication are often difficult to determine. When a copyright, or other date is not printed on the card, an educated guess is made based on postmark and the style of postcard. When the dates cannot be reasonably determined they are omitted.

c. 1908, Publisher unknown [$10-12]

c. 1909, E. Nash, New York, NY [$10-12]

© 1908, International Art Publishing Co., New York, NY [$10-12]

Chapter 1
Humble Beginnings
(1809–1831)

Nancy Hanks, the wife of Thomas Lincoln, gave birth to her second child on a cold Sunday morning. The date was February 12, 1809. Little could she have realized that the son she brought into the world on that day would go on to determine the fate of the nation. This child of destiny was named Abraham, after his paternal grandfather, who in 1786 had been killed by Native Americans while working in his fields. Young Abraham's father, Thomas, was a man who provided for his family by using his skills as a carpenter, doing odd jobs and farming. In 1808 he purchased a 300 acre tract of land, named the Sinking Spring Farm, for $200 cash. It was located on Nolin Creek, just about three miles from Hodgenville, Kentucky. Here he built a one room log cabin, 18 feet wide and 16 feet long, with just a single window and a dirt packed floor. This was to be the birthplace of the man who would become the 16th President of the United States.

A VIEW OF THE LINCOLN BIRTHPLACE FARM
From the spot where the cabin stands

Copyrighted, 1909, by The Lincoln Farm Association.

This is a view of the farmland at the site of Sinking Spring Farm on Nolin Creek in Hardin County, Kentucky, where Abraham Lincoln was born.
© *1909, Lincoln Farm Association [$4-6]*

This early 19th century log cabin, symbolic of the one in which Lincoln was born, has been carefully preserved. Purchased on land close to the original home site by Alfred W. Dennett in 1894, it was put on display as the actual birth cabin. In fact, it probably only contains a few of the original logs from the Lincoln cabin, as the Lincoln cabin had apparently been moved and rebuilt after the family had relocated. Today the cabin is on display inside a special memorial building on the original farm acreage.
c. 1935, Curteich, Chicago, IL [$2-4]

LINCOLN CABIN, INSIDE MEMORIAL HALL ON LINCOLN FARM, NEAR HODGENVILLE, KY.

A one room log cabin, located about three miles from Hodgenville, Kentucky, was the birthplace of Abraham Lincoln. He would live the first two years of his life in this cabin, which measured 16 by 18 feet.
© 1908, M.W. Taggart, New York, NY [$6-8]

Lincoln spent his young life living in one rustic log cabin home after another. It wasn't until he settled in Springfield, Illinois, as an adult, that this changed. He would later become known as the "Log Cabin President."
© 1908, Julius Bien & Co., New York, NY [$8-12]

Standing only a few hundred yards from the family's cabin was a large white oak tree known as the "Boundary Oak". Marking one corner of the property, it was estimated to have been about 300 years old at the time of Lincoln's birth. Today only the base of the tree remains.
1946, Curteich, Chicago, IL [$2-4]

Between the years 1811-1816 the Lincolns
lived in a cabin on the 230 acre Knob Creek
Farm, near Hodgenville. This is a reconstruction of that cabin.
1957, Curteich, Chicago, IL [$2-4]

What little formal education Lincoln received in his lifetime
began in a small, one room log schoolhouse, not far from the
family cabin. During the fall of 1815, he and his sister Sarah,
attended this A.B.C. school taught by Zachariah Riney.
Dexter Press, Pearl River, NY [$1-3]

After years of neglect the gravesite of Nancy
Hanks Lincoln was overgrown with vegetation
and its exact position lost. After the assassination of her son, a concentrated effort relocated
her grave. In 1879 a headstone was placed at
the spot to mark its location.
Walter H. Miller & Co., Williamsburg, VA [$2-4]

The Lincolns moved about 10 miles away to a new, more
productive farm, when Abe was just two years old. It would
be this 230 acre farm at Knob Creek that Abe Lincoln would
remember years later as an adult. Shortly after settling here,
in 1812, a younger brother Thomas was born. He would
die sometime in infancy. Like most youngsters of his time,
Abe spent his days doing chores, helping with the planting,
roaming the woods, and otherwise enjoying life as a frontier
child. In the fall of 1815, at the age of six, he attended school
for a few weeks with his older sister Sarah. This began his
formal education. The school, taught by Zachariah Riney and
later Caleb Hazel, was located about two miles northeast of
the family cabin.

In December, 1816, the Lincolns once again moved to a
new homestead. This time they journeyed 91 miles, crossing
the Ohio River and settling on land near Little Pigeon Creek in
present day Spencer County, Indiana. Here his father taught
young Abe, eight years old and large for his age, how to
use an ax. He would soon master the use of this tool, and
until he reached the age of 23 would seldom be without
it. His father put him to work assisting him in clearing and
farming the land.

On October 5, 1818 tragedy struck, when Abe's mother
Nancy died from "milk sickness." This illness was caused by
drinking milk from cows that had eaten the poisonous white
snakeroot plant. It was an ailment all too common on the
frontier. So it was that at nine years of age, young Abraham
was called upon to help make his beloved mother's coffin.
In the words of his cousin and best friend, Dennis Hanks,
Nancy Lincoln had taught Abe "goodness, kindness, read the
good Bible to him, taught him to read and to spell, taught
him sweetness and benevolence as well." Her death was a
severe blow to the small family. Sarah, at the age of 12, had
to take over the responsibilities of running the household.

On this site, known as the Little Pigeon Creek Farm, Thomas Lincoln purchased 160 acres of land. This is a replica of the cabin that young, eight year old Abe, helped his father build. The Lincoln family would live on this farm for 14 years.
Walter H. Miller & Co., Williamsburg, VA [$2-4]

Lincoln's mother sent him off to receive some schooling at the age of six. The school, about two miles away was where he learned his ABC's and basic numbers. His mother encouraged his learning.
c. 1950s, Publisher unknown [$2-4]

LINCOLN and MOTHER

Grave of Nancy Hanks Lincoln, Lincoln City, Indiana

In October, 1818, Lincoln's mother died from "milk sickness." She was buried in a simple pine coffin made from trees on the property. A gravesite was chosen just a short distance from the family's cabin and there she was laid to rest without the benefit of a religious ceremony.
c. 1910, Souvenir Postcard Co., Rockford, IL [$4-6]

While living at Pigeon Creek, Lincoln received some of his basic education by attending one room school houses like that seen here. This reconstruction is found at the Lincoln Pioneer Village in Rockport, Indiana. George Honig, the man behind construction of the village, is seen looking into the school building.
c. 1935, Publisher unknown [$10-12]

Young Abe Lincoln spent many hours before the fire at night reading and ciphering. He once remarked, "the things I want to know are in books; my best friend is the man who'll get me a book I ain't read."
c. 1940, The Kyle Co., Louisville, KY [$2-4]

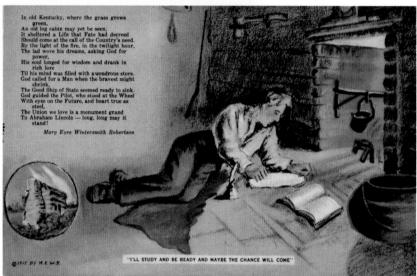

In old Kentucky, where the grass grows green,
An old log cabin may yet be seen,
It sheltered a Life that Fate had decreed
Should come at the call of the Country's need.
By the light of the fire, in the twilight hour,
The lad wove his dreams, asking God for power,
His soul longed for wisdom and drank in rich lore
Til his mind was filled with a wondrous store.
God called for a Man when the bravest might shrink,
The Good Ship of State seemed ready to sink.
God guided the Pilot, who stood at the Wheel
With eyes on the Future, and heart true as steel,
The Union we love is a monument grand
To Abraham Lincoln — long, long may it stand!

Mary Eyre Wintersmith Robertson

"I'LL STUDY AND BE READY AND MAYBE THE CHANCE WILL COME"

A little over one year after his wife had died, Thomas took a trip back to Elizabethtown, Kentucky, where he had previously lived. There he looked up a woman whom he had courted briefly before marrying Nancy Hanks. Sarah Bush Johnston was a widow with three children of her own. Thomas proposed, she accepted, and they were wed on December 2, 1819. Returning to the Pigeon Creek cabin, this new family, plus an orphaned cousin Dennis Hanks, set up house. Now eight people occupied the small cabin. Sarah Lincoln, commonly known as "Sally," soon got the homestead cleaned up, organized, and running smoothly. Sally was a very kind hearted woman who quickly endeared herself to the young Lincoln children. Unable to read or write herself, she nevertheless encouraged Abe to pursue his education.

In 1820 he attended school again for several months. This was a "blab" school kept by Andrew Crawford. A "blab" school employed a method of teaching by which all of the students recited their lessons together. Later, Lincoln would go to a similar school run by James Swaney. At the age 17, his final academic instruction was with schoolmaster Azel Dorsey. All together, the total formal education that Abraham received amounted to about one year of schooling. However, he had an incredibly strong desire to read and learn. He began to read every book in the community and its surroundings, for miles around. Among his favorites were the family *Bible, Aesop's Fables, Pilgrim's Progress, Robinson Crusoe,* works by Shakespeare, and *The Life of George Washington*. The book on Washington, borrowed from a neighbor, was accidentally damaged by rain while in his possession. To pay for this book he worked off its value with three days of labor. This would be the first book that Lincoln would personally own.

This painting by Norman Rockwell shows Lincoln as he might have looked before heading out on his own, at the age of 22. Abe always took a book with him wherever he went, so that he could do some reading whenever the opportunity arose.
Litho-Art Printers Inc., Spokane, WA [$4-6]

Starting at the age of eight, when his father put an ax in his hands to help in the building of the family cabin, Abe Lincoln began developing his skills with this important tool. As a young man he would often hire himself out to split fence rails for his neighbors.
© 1908, M.W. Taggart, New York, NY [$8-10]

For most of his teenage years, Abraham was kept busy clearing land, splitting logs, cutting firewood, and farming. He would often carry a book in his pocket to read whenever the opportunity arose. His preference for reading, ciphering, and book learning over manual labor sometimes created problems between himself and his father. When the workday was done, Abe and his cousin Dennis Hanks, often walked to the nearby town of Gentryville. At the country store there they would sit around with other farm boys and swap jokes and stories. This was where Abe honed his skills as a storyteller and many came to listen to his yarns.

On January 28, 1828, tragedy once again struck when Abe's sister Sarah, who had married in 1826, died in childbirth shortly before her 21st birthday. That spring, merchant James Gentry hired Abe to take a flatboat of goods to New Orleans. Accompanying him on the 1,200 mile trip was Gentry's son, Allen. New Orleans was the first real city that Lincoln ever saw, and it was an eye-opening experience.

Returning almost three months later, by steamboat, he learned that the family would shortly be on the move again. On March 1, 1830, with three wagons filled with their possessions, the Lincolns set out for their new home. Some 225 miles later they reached the north bank of the Sangamon River, about 10 miles from Decatur, Illinois. There they built a new cabin in which to live.

After the crops had been planted Abe hired out to split fence rails for neighbors. During this period of time he split thousands of fence rails, earning himself the nickname "the rail splitter." It was in 1830 that Lincoln made his first political speech, advocating that improvements be made for navigation on the Sangamon River. The next spring Thomas proceeded to move the family one last time. They migrated on to Goose Nest Prairie in Coles County. At this point, Abraham decided to leave the family and set out on his own.

A neighbor for whom he once worked said of him "Abe could sink an ax deeper in wood then any man I ever saw." Abe certainly had plenty of practice, as he split many thousands of fence rails in his youth. © *1908, E. Nash, New York, NY [$10-12]*

In 1829, Thomas Lincoln, with the help of his son Abraham, built this cabin on the Little Pigeon Creek Farm to replace the one the family had been living in for years. Only a short time later, before it was completely finished, the family moved to a new homestead in Illinois. This is how the cabin looked years after the Lincolns had left the area. Although taken down in 1874, the bottom logs of the cabin were cast in bronze and are now on display at the Lincoln Boyhood National Memorial.
1931, Curteich, Chicago, IL [$3-5]

Abe left his family in 1831 to begin life on his own. Before doing so, he helped his father erect this log cabin on Gooseneck Prairie in Coles County, Illinois.
c. 1909, Hammon Publishing Co., Chicago, IL [$4-6]

An interior view of the cabin shows a spinning wheel said to have been used by Lincoln's stepmother.
c. 1910, Hammon Publishing Co., Chicago, IL [$4-6]

Chapter Two

Road to the White House
(1832–1860)

Beginning a new life in the spring of 1831, Abe made his second trip to New Orleans. On this occasion it was businessman Denton Offutt who hired him, along with his cousin John Hanks and stepbrother John Johnston, to take a flatboat down to the port city. Lincoln left for the trip to New Orlean from the small town of Sangmo Town. His flatboat got hung up on Rutledge's mill damn in the town of New Salem. After freeing the boat from the dam, Lincoln and his companions continued downstream to New Orleans. While in the city Abe witnessed first hand a slave auction. Legend has it that after observing the mistreatment and degradation of an attractive mulatto girl, he turned to his companions and exclaimed, "if ever I get a chance to hit that thing [meaning slavery], I'll hit it hard."

When returning north in July, Lincoln stopped in New Salem in late July, as he would later say, "a piece of floating driftwood." Without a job and on his own, Lincoln was looking for new opportunities. His first opportunity arose when Denton Offutt, having been impressed with this young man, hired him to clerk in a general store that he had just opened in New Salem. Managing Offutt's store gave Abe a chance to swap stories with customers, discuss politics, and continue his passion for reading.

Lincoln boarded for a time at the Rutledge Tavern, where he met the innkeeper's daughter, Ann. Legend has it that Ann Rutledge was his first love and that he had actually proposed to her. The truth of this matter has been a subject of debate among historians. At the very least they were likely close friends.

Offutt's store did not do well financially and was forced to close in 1832. It was at this point that Abe decided to run for public office. Before he could pursue his political ambitions the Black Hawk War broke out. This conflict began when Black Hawk, the leader of the Saux and Fox tribes, invaded Illinois with about 500 armed warriors creating havoc among the settlers. The state militia was called up and Abe enlisted. Elected captain, he was to serve for only a few months before things settled down and he returned to New Salem without seeing any combat. Once back home in July, he began campaigning again for a seat in the Illinois State Legislature. He was unsuccessful in the election, coming in eighth in a field of 13 candidates.

READING LAW.

"If I ever get a chance to hit that thing [slavery], I'll hit it hard."—*Lincoln's remark on coming out of a slave market, at New Orleans.*

LINCOLN DURING HIS PRESIDENCY.
From a photograph by Brady.

LINCOLN IN THE SLAVE MARKET.

Copyright, 1908, BY THE CENTURY CO.

During the spring of 1831 Lincoln and two of his relatives were hired by Denton Offutt to take a flatboat of goods to New Orleans. On this, his second trip to that city, he witnessed the proceedings of a slave auction. This experience helped to deepen his antislavery sentiments.
1908, The Century Co., New York, NY [$6-8]

Denton Offutt and Lincoln built this small log cabin store in New Salem in August, 1831. Lincoln was hired to clerk the store, which was only in business for eight months.
c. 1930, Herbert Georg Studio, Chicago, IL [$6-8]

The Rutledge Tavern was built in 1828 by James Rutledge, a co-founder of New Salem. It is probably where Lincoln, who lodged here, first met Ann Rutledge.
1939, Curteich, Chicago, IL [$2-4]

Lincoln & Berry Store, Lincoln State Park, Petersburg, Ill.

In August, 1832 after failing to be re-elected to the Illinois State Legislature, Lincoln became partners with William Berry in a general store. They purchased the store on credit. Here Lincoln swapped stories and talked politics with the locals. When a larger store became available across the street, he and Berry bought it and moved their business. This is a reconstruction of that first store on its original site.
c. 1928, Auburn Post Card Mfg. Co., Auburn, IN [$2-4]

After his political defeat, Abe entered into a partnership in 1832 with William F. Berry who had served with him in the militia. They borrowed money to buy a store owned by James and Rowan Herndon. The general store sold dry goods and was a place where people would gather to swap stories and talk politics. In January, 1833, Berry and Lincoln purchased and moved into a larger store across the street that had been owned by Reuben Radford. For a period of time, Abe used the lean-to storeroom, attached to the back of the store, as his bedroom. Despite the fact that people loved to come to hear Abe's storytelling, the store did not do well and the partners just got deeper into debt. As Abe would later say, "the store winked out." Thus ended his career as a storekeeper.

On May 7, 1833, shortly before the failure of the store, President Andrew Jackson appointed Lincoln postmaster. He held this office for three years, earning himself an average of $3.00 a day. About this time the county surveyor agreed to make Abe his assistant. So purchasing the needed equipment on credit and studying hard, he taught himself the art of surveying in six weeks. This earned him an additional $3.00 a day which helped him to pay down his debts.

The summer of 1834 saw Abe once again pursuing politics. He became the Whig Party candidate for the state legislature and was elected in August to what would be the first of four terms. Serving in the House gave him insight into the inner workings of government and politics. During the campaign, one of the state's political leaders, John T. Stuart, encouraged him to begin studying the law. Lending Abe his law books, he stressed that the way to become successful in politics was by becoming a lawyer. When the legislature adjourned in February, 1835, Abe took to studying the law with great fervor. On August 25 of that same year he would receive the sad news that Ann Rutledge, with whom folklore has linked him romantically, had died at the age of 22.

Lincoln and Berry moved into their second store in mid January of 1833. This is a reconstruction of that store located in New Salem State Park.
c. 1940, L.L. Cook Co., Milwaukee, WI [$6-8]

This postcard view shows a diorama depicting Lincoln as storekeeper in the second Lincoln-Berry store. He is seen waiting on Ann Rutledge, with whom legend has linked him romantically.
Artvue Post Card Co., New York, NY [$4-6]

On May 7, 1833 Lincoln was appointed postmaster of New Salem, a post he held until May 30, 1836. This is a restored version of the interior of the Lincoln-Berry store, which also served as the post office.
1956, Curteich, Chicago, IL [$3-5]

This is the Lincoln-Berry store as it may have looked in 1833. Here all manner of general merchandise was sold. Unfortunately, as Lincoln would later say, the store just "winked out," leaving him $1,100 in debt. This debt took him 15 years to repay.
Herbert Georg Studios [$4-6]

BERRY-LINCOLN STORE, LEAN-TO WHERE LINCOLN SLEPT

Attached to the back of the store was a lean-to, which served both as a storeroom and, for a period of time, Lincoln's bedroom.
Herbert Georg Studios [$4-6]

Ann Rutledge's Grave, Lincoln's First Love, Petersburg, Illinois

Ann Rutledge died on August 25, 1835 and was buried in Old Concord Cemetery, not far from New Salem. In 1890 some of her remains were exhumed and reburied in Oakland Cemetery in nearby Petersburg.
c. 1906, George F. Luthringer, Petersburg, IL [$4-6]

THE OLD ABE LINCOLN LOG COURT HOUSE, DECATUR, ILL.

Lincoln first saw this courthouse in Decatur, Illinois when he arrived here in mid March, 1830. He later practiced law here in 1838 as part of his judicial circuit.
c. 1916, Wait-Cahill Co., Decatur, IL [$3-5]

From 1837-1876 this building served as the Illinois State House and Supreme Court Building. Lincoln pleaded 243 or more cases here before the court. He also served his last term in the State Legislature, 1840-1841, in this building. On June 16, 1858, he delivered his famous "House Divided" speech to the Republican State Convention held in the House chamber. During the years 1876-1966 the building was utilized as the Sangamon County Courthouse.
Grogan Photo, Danville, IL [$3-5]

Sangamon County Court House
SPRINGFIELD, ILLINOIS

LINCOLN COURT HOUSE · RE-ERECTED IN GREENFIELD VILLAGE · DEARBORN, MICHIGAN

Built in 1840 in Pottsville (now Lincoln, Illinois), this courthouse was where Lincoln tried a number of cases between the years 1840-1847. The original structure was dismantled and rebuilt in Greenfield Village, Dearborn, Michigan.
c. 1930, Artcraft Photo Co., East Rutherford, NJ [$4-5]

In 1836, Lincoln was re-elected to the Illinois House of Representatives for the second time. During this term in office, he was instrumental in getting the state's capital moved from Vandalia to Springfield. Between sessions of the House he continued to supplement his income by surveying. This was to change when he received his license to practice law on September 9, at the age of 28. On March 1, 1837, he was admitted to the Illinois Bar. Now, after much self-study, he was a lawyer.

On April 1, 1837 he left New Salem and moved to Springfield where he formed his first law partnership with his mentor John T. Stuart. At that time, Springfield had a population of 1,500 and was growing quickly. However, the courts in Springfield were only in session for a few weeks each year. To further increase his practice, Lincoln began "riding the circuit." This meant traveling and practicing law in several central Illinois counties. Each year, during spring and fall, he would cover over 12,000 square miles in the Eighth Judicial Circuit. During his career as a lawyer Lincoln eventually handled upwards of 5,000 cases. In doing so he gained a reputation for honesty and integrity, just as he had, when he was younger.

The Edward's home where A. Lincoln and Mary Todd were married Nov. 4, 1842.

Mary Todd Lincoln and Abraham Lincoln were married in this house owned by Ninian Edwards. The ceremony took place on the evening of November 4, 1842. At the time, Mary was living here with her sister and brother-in-law. This was also the house in which Mary died on July 16, 1882.
c. 1920, Publisher unknown [$18-20]

Interior of Room where A. Lincoln & Mary Todd were married Nov. 4, 1842.

A view of the room in which the Reverend Charles Dresser married the Lincolns. About 30 guests were present for the ceremony.
c. 1920, Publisher unknown [$18-20]

Abe ran again for the state House in 1838 and once more was victorious. When the State Legislature moved to the new capital of Springfield, on December 9, 1839, he was present. To honor this occasion, a cotillion ball was held at the home of Ninian Edwards located across the street from the new capitol building. Here Abe met a 21 year-old young woman named Mary Todd, from Lexington, Kentucky, who had come to Springfield to live with her sister, the wife of Ninian Edwards.

Coming from a well-to-do family with high social standing, her background was much different than that of Lincoln. The chance meeting led to a courtship between this unlikely couple and, later, to an engagement to marry. A date was set for January 1, 1841. When that day arrived however, Abe did not show. He had misgivings and serious doubts about marriage.

For months he was despondent and melancholy, grappling with what to do about the situation. To his law partner, John Stuart he wrote, "I am now the most miserable man living. If what I feel were equally distributed to the whole human family, there would not be one cheerful face on earth."

In April, 1841, his partnership with Stuart was mutually dissolved and he quickly started a new one with Stephen T. Logan. He worked diligently at his law practice while trying to solve his personal dilemma with Mary. Eventually a mutual friend brought them back together and they worked out their problems. Then on the evening of November 4, 1842, they were married at the home of Ninian Edwards. In the presence of a few close friends and family members, Abe placed a ring on Mary's finger engraved with the words, "Love is Eternal." They would be married for 22 years and 162 days.

MRS. ABRAHAM LINCOLN

This photograph of Mary Todd Lincoln was probably taken very early in 1862. Mary disliked having her picture taken, and because of the difference in their heights, never posed with her husband.
© 1907, Buckingham & Harley, Washington, D.C. [$15-20]

This portrait of Mary Lincoln was painted by Francis B. Carpenter. It was to be a present from many to her husband. However he was assassinated before receiving it.
Laura N. Goldberg, Hazel Park, MI [$2-3]

Purchased for $1,500 on May 2, 1844 from the Rev. Charles Dresser, this was the only home ever owned by the Lincolns. Over the years they enlarged and made improvements to the house until it looked as it does here.
c. 1905, Illustrated Postal Card Co., New York, NY [$4-6]

This is an interior view of one of the rooms in the Lincoln home.
c. 1910, Hammon Publishing Co., Chicago, IL [$4-6]

After they married the Lincolns moved into the Globe Tavern. They took a room on the second floor at a cost of $4.00 a week. It was here on August 1, 1843, that Mary gave birth to their first child, Robert Todd Lincoln. Not long after, they rented a larger three room cottage at 214 South Fourth Street. At the time Abe was making a good living as a lawyer, earning between $1,200 and $1,500 a year. By 1844 he was able to pay off the debts that he had accumulated in New Salem and had enough left to buy his own home. The house he and Mary purchased for $1,500 was situated on the corner of Eighth and Jackson Streets. A one and a half story house, it would be the only home they would ever own. Later, in 1856, they would spend an additional $1,300 to enlarge the house to a full two stories. They moved into this dwelling in May, 1844.

The Lincoln home sits on the northeast corner of Eighth and Jackson Streets. Restored to its appearance in 1860, it is now a National Historic Site. Visitors are welcome to tour the home where the family lived from 1844-1861.
Es-N-Len Photos, Aurora, IL [$2-3]

At the end of the year Abe dissolved his law partnership with Stephen T. Logan. He then entered what would be his last law practice with a man nine years his junior, William H. Herndon. Later Herndon would go on to write a famous biography of his friend and partner. On March 10, 1846, the Lincoln's second son, Edward Baker Lincoln (called "Eddie"), was born.

Following his political ambitions, Lincoln ran for the United States House of Representatives in 1846. At the age of 39 he was elected to Congress and he and his family rented out their home and headed to Washington, D.C. In Washington they rented rooms at Mrs. Spriggs' boarding house, just east of the capitol. As a congressman, Lincoln questioned the need for the Mexican War, and also tried to get a law passed eliminating slavery in the District of Columbia. Neither of these stands made him popular back home in Illinois. When his term in office was over, he returned to Springfield where he campaigned on behalf of Zachary Taylor who was running for president. After Taylor won the election, Lincoln was offered the job of governor of the Oregon Territory. He turned this proposition down and resumed his career as a lawyer once again.

Soon he was gaining a reputation as one of the best lawyers in the state and had a steadily increasing practice. Not only did he continue making the usual court circuits, but he also argued cases in Federal Court and before the State Supreme Court.

But once again death would strike close. After 52 days of illness, young Edward Lincoln, not quite four years old, died on February 1, 1850. The death struck Mary especially hard and she shut herself inside her bedroom for weeks. Later that same year, on December 21, they were blessed with the birth of their third son, William Wallace Lincoln, known as "Willie." Three years later, Thomas, the fourth and last of the Lincoln children, was born on April 4, 1853. Thomas was nicknamed "Tad" by his father, who said that Tad's large head reminded him of a tadpole.

Lincoln pressed on with his law practice, while still keeping a hand in politics. He was re-elected once again to the Illinois State Legislature, but he quickly gave up the post when the chance to seek election to the United States Senate arose. His attempt at gaining the senate seat ended in failure. A year later he appeared at the organizational meeting for the Republican Party held in Bloomington, Illinois. It's here that he delivered a well known oration called the "Lost Speech." At the first Republican Party National Convention in Philadelphia, on June 14, 1856, he received 110 votes for vice-president. This was just short of what he needed to capture a spot on the national ticket with the presidential candidate John C. Fremont. Lincoln then went on to deliver over 50 speeches in support of Fremont.

Court House, Beardstown, Ill.

It was here at the Courthouse in Beardstown, Indiana, that Lincoln argued one of his most famous cases. On May 7, 1858 he successfully defended his client, Duff Armstrong, in a murder trial by utilizing an almanac to discredit an "eyewitness." The results were widely publicized and helped Lincoln gain a reputation as a skilled lawyer.
1936, Curteich, Chicago, IL [$4-6]

The year 1858 would be an eventful one for Lincoln both as a lawyer and as a politician. On May 7, Lincoln cleared a client, "Duff" Armstrong of murder charges, by discrediting the star witness against him. The witness claimed to have seen Armstrong kill a man under the light of a bright full moon. Abe proved the testimony was false by using an almanac to show that the night in question was actually pitch black. This case made big news in the state and added to Lincoln's fame as a lawyer.

In his political life, Lincoln was the one and only choice of the Republican Party to run for the United States Senate in 1858. In accepting his nomination he delivered his famous "House Divided" speech. It was in this speech that he uttered these prophetic words, "A house divided against itself cannot stand. I believe this government cannot endure permanently half slave and half free…It will become all one thing, or all the other." This brought his name to national attention. His political opponent for the senate seat was Stephen A. Douglas, nicknamed the "little giant," who was the incumbent senator. On August 21, 1858, the first of seven celebrated debates took place between these two men in Ottawa, Illinois. Others were held in the towns of Freeport, Jonesboro, Charleston, Galesburg, Quincy, and Alton. During the campaign Lincoln gave at least 63 speeches throughout the state. In the end he lost to Douglas, but through this series of debates, and the election itself, Lincoln gained important national recognition that would serve him well in the future.

The Illinois Republican Party nominated Lincoln as their candidate for the United States Senate on June 16, 1858. This began a campaign that involved traveling thousands of miles, crisscrossing the state, delivering his political message.
c. 1909, The Rose Co., Philadelphia, PA [$10-12]

The second of the famous Lincoln-Douglas debates took place August 27, 1858, in Freeport, Illinois. Lincoln arrived in a conestoga wagon pulled by six white horses. A crowd of 15,000 people heard the two men express their views on the issue of slavery.
1944, Chicago Historical Society, Chicago, IL [$3-5]

On October 7, 1858, Lincoln and Douglas met in Galesburg, Illinois. Here they spoke from a platform located on the east side of Knox College's Old Main Building. The momentous event is shown in this painting by the artist Ralph Fletcher Seymour.
c. 1955, Curteich, Chicago, IL [$3-5]

Abraham Lincoln and Stephen A. Douglas

During the senate campaign of 1858 Lincoln challenged his political opponent, Stephen A. Douglas, to a series of seven debates to be held at various sites around the state. These men would later oppose each other in the 1860 presidential election.
Publisher unknown [$4-6]

The debate at Knox College, the fifth in the series, drew an estimated 10,000 people. Nationwide attention was drawn to both men as the newspapers reprinted and widely circulated their spoken words. What caught most people's attention were their opposing views on the issue of slavery.
1958, Curteich, Chicago, IL [$4-6]

COMMEMORATING
The Lincoln-Douglas Debate
KNOX COLLEGE   1858-1958 GALESBURG, ILLINOIS

KNOX COLLEGE FOR LINCOLN

" . . . there is but one path to peace . . . allowing each State to decide for itself whether it wants slavery or not."
—Douglas

Joint Debate Oct. 7th 1858

" . . . he is blowing out the moral lights around us, when he contends that whoever wants slaves has a right to hold them."
—Lincoln

1809—LINCOLN CENTENARY—1909

INDIANA HOME.

If any personal description of me is thought desirable, it may be said I am, in height, six feet four inches, nearly; lean in flesh, weighing on an average one hundred and eighty pounds; dark complexion, with coarse black hair and gray eyes. No other marks or brands recollected. *—From a brief autobiography.*

LINCOLN AT THE TIME HE MADE THE COOPER UNION SPEECH.
From a photograph by Brady, February, 1860.

COOPER UNION.

Copyright, 1908, BY THE CENTURY CO.

This photograph of Lincoln was taken at Mathew Brady's Broadway Studio on the day of the Cooper Union speech. The success of his address helped convince many in his political party that he would make a good choice for a presidential candidate.
1908, The Century Co., New York, NY [$5-7]

At the Cooper Union Hall in New York City, Lincoln addressed some 1,500 people. The speech, given on the evening of February 27, 1860, brought high praise from those in attendance.
Publisher unknown [$4-6]

LINCOLN

Campaign picture, made by Hesler in Springfield, June 3, 1860

New York's Cooper Union Great Hall

Mary Todd Lincoln
1818 - 1882

Some of the most important people, including the editors of the major newspapers of New York City, gathered to hear a speech at the Cooper Union building on February 27, 1860. The person they came to hear deliver that speech was Abraham Lincoln. Beginning rather poorly at first, Lincoln nevertheless went on to captivate his audience of 1,500 people for nearly one and a half hours. He argued that slavery should not be extended to the new territories and that the founding fathers of our nation had had anti-slavery intentions. But, Lincoln also conceded that there should be no interference with slavery where it now existed. Republicans, he said, should not compromise on this issue of opposing the extension of slavery. With the words, "Let us have faith that right makes might, and in that faith let us, to the end, dare to do our duty as we understand it," he ended the speech. Winning over his listeners, he received a prolonged standing ovation. In response, the *New York Tribune* newspaper later printed the full text of the speech. The success of this speech helped to push Lincoln into the forefront of the Republican Party.

The Chicago "Wigwam" was the site of the 1860 Republican National Convention. Erected on the southeast corner of Lake and Market Streets (later Wacker Drive), it was meant to be a temporary structure. Costing $5000, the two story building, made entirely of wood, could hold 12,000 people.
Dexter Press, West Nyack, NY [$2-4]

The Republican Convention, held in Chicago on May 18, 1860, resulted in Abraham Lincoln being selected as the party's presidential candidate. This occurred on the third ballot when the Ohio delegation changed their votes in favor of Lincoln, giving him the necessary votes to become the nominee.
c. 1950, Publisher unknown [$4-6]

Not surprisingly, his name was brought up three months later, at the Republican National Convention in Chicago, as a possible presidential nominee. On the third ballot, taken on May 18, 1860, he became the official Republican candidate for president. In the Democratic Party things became complicated when the party split and nominated two candidates. The Northern wing of the party selected Stephen A. Douglas as their nominee, while the Southern slave favoring faction chose John C. Breckinridge. Also thrown into this mixture was the candidate John Bell of the newly formed Constitutional Party. With four candidates splitting the vote it was almost certain that Lincoln would win the election.

On May 19, 1860 a delegation of important Republicans, arrived in Springfield from the Chicago Convention, and called on Lincoln at his home. There they presented him with the formal notification that he was chosen as his party's candidate for the presidency.
1944, Chicago Historical Society, Chicago, IL [$3-5]

This postcard features a diorama depicting the June 7 campaign rally staged by various delegations of the Republican Party to honor Lincoln's nomination. Held in front of the Lincoln home in Springfield, it was an all day affair. There was an eight mile long procession in the morning, speeches during the afternoon and evening, and a torch light parade to finish the celebrations.
1944, Chicago Historical Society, Chicago, IL [$3-5]

Even before the election was held, some leaders in the Southern states began to urge secession in the event that Lincoln was victorious. Election day held on November 6, 1860, would prove to be a pivotal election in our nation's history. The results were that Lincoln received only 40% of the popular vote, while his opponents had out polled him by almost one million votes. This was enough, however, to garner 180 of the 303 possible electoral votes. It was by these circumstances that Abraham Lincoln, at the age of 52, was elected the 16th President of the United States.

After Lincoln's election became a reality, South Carolina broke from the Union on December 20, 1860. This was followed quickly in January by the secession of the states of Mississippi, Florida, Alabama, Georgia, and Louisiana. Shortly after, Texas joined this confederacy, with several other states on the verge of banding with them. Ultimately, a total of 11 states broke from the Union. On February 4, 1861, representatives of these states met and formed the Confederate States of America. Jefferson Davis was elected president of this newly formed separate government, with Alexander H. Stephens his vice-president. Thus the stage was being set for the great pending conflict.

During the 1860 presidential campaign, this painting, titled *Lincoln the Rail Splitter*, was often used at Republican Party rallies. It promoted Lincoln as a backwoods, honest, hardworking candidate. The painting by an unknown artist is in the Chicago Historical Society's collection.
Arthur Jaffe Heliochrome Co., New York, NY [$4-6]

Patriotic campaign banners such as this one were used to help promote Abraham Lincoln's candidacy for president.
c. 1950s, Publisher unknown [$4-6]

This wax representation of Abraham Lincoln depicts him as he looked during the presidential campaign. His likeness was created from a life mask and hand models made in the summer of 1860. Lincoln did not grow a beard until after the election. He was the first president to have one.
c. 1960, Springfield News Agency, Springfield, IL [$2-4]

Chapter 3

The Presidency & the Civil War

(1861–1865)

Having now been elected to the presidency, Lincoln prepared to leave his home in Springfield. He rented his home for $350 a year, sold most of his furniture, and packed up the family's belongings. On February 11, 1861 the Lincolns boarded a special train to begin what would be a 12-day journey to Washington, D.C. Just before departing from the station, Abe spoke from the platform of the rear car to the crowd that had gathered to see him off. Among his words to the people of Springfield he said, "To this place, and the kindness of these people, I owe everything…to His care commending you, as I hope in your prayers you will commend me, I bid you an affectionate farewell."

CHICAGO HISTORICAL SOCIETY

LEAVING SPRINGFIELD FOR WASHINGTON, 1861

48187-N

At 8 a.m. on the morning of February 11, 1861 the Lincolns boarded the train to depart Springfield for Washington D.C. Before leaving, Lincoln gave a short, but emotional speech to the approximately 1,000 people gathered to wish him a fond farewell.
1944, Chicago Historical Society, Chicago, IL [$3-5]

During his trip from Springfield to Washington, D.C. for his inauguration, Lincoln stopped briefly in Lancaster, Pennsylvania, on the morning of February 22, 1861. There he delivered some brief remarks at the Caldwell House Hotel before proceeding to Harrisburg.
c. 1960s, Stel-Mar, Lancaster, PA [$2-4]

After giving a speech to the State House in Harrisburg, Pennsylvania, Lincoln left the city clandestinely to continue his trip on to the nation's capital.
c. 1909, P. Sander, New York, NY [$12-15]

The trip to Washington involved passing through many cities and towns, often stopping to make a public appearance or deliver a short speech. This circuitous route was planned so that as many people as possible might see and hear their new president. Eventually he reached Philadelphia on February 21. While in this city Lincoln received word from the private detective Allan Pinkerton, that there was a plot to murder him when he passed through Baltimore. The next day he participated in a flag raising ceremony at Independence Hall and proclaimed "in my view of the present aspect of affairs, there is no need of bloodshed and war." From there he traveled on to Harrisburg, the state capital of Pennsylvania.

In Harrisburg a plan was devised to secretly transport the president-elect to Washington. Lincoln changed from his normal clothing and donned an overcoat as a disguise. Then, accompanied by his friend Ward Hill Laman and detective Allan Pinkerton, boarded a train unannounced. As further insurance, all of the telegraph lines leading out of Harrisburg were cut. In this manner they successfully passed through Baltimore undetected and arrived in the nation's capital at 6 o'clock in the morning.

Lincoln was sworn in as the 16th President of the United States by Chief Justice Roger B. Taney on March 4, 1861. *c. 1910, Raphael Tuck & Sons, London, England {$12-15]*

President Lincoln is shown here with portraits of Vice-President Hannibal Hamlin and the rest of his cabinet. Included is Edwin Stanton who replaced Simon Cameron as Secretary of War in January, 1862. *Authentic Distributors Inc., Massapequa, NY [$6-8]*

At noon on March 4, 1861 President James Buchanan arrived at Willard's Hotel to accompany Lincoln to the inauguration ceremonies. Together they rode in an open carriage in the procession that headed down Pennsylvania Avenue. Along the route soldiers lined the street and mounted cavalry were stationed at every street crossing. All this was in fear that Southern sympathizers might try to interrupt the proceedings. Upon reaching the temporary platform set up at the east portico of the unfinished Capitol building, Lincoln watched as his vice-president, Hannibal Hamlin was sworn in. Then he stood before the expectant crowd that had gathered and delivered his first inaugural address. In the speech, which lasted about 30 minutes, he reaffirmed his intentions of not wishing to interfere with the institution of slavery where it already existed. He appealed to the Southern states for calm, stating "In your hands, my dissatisfied fellow countrymen, and not in mine, is the momentous issue of civil war...we are not enemies, but friends. We must not be enemies." When he had finished, the Chief Justice of the Supreme Court administered the oath of office. Abraham Lincoln was now president of the United States.

Fort Sumter, located in Charleston Harbor, South Carolina is where the Civil War began. At 4:30 a.m. on April 12, 1861 Confederate shore batteries shelled the fort for a day and a half before it was forced to surrender.
c. 1910, The Valentine & Sons Publishing Co., New York, NY [$3-5]

The first night of his presidency, Lincoln received a report from Major Robert Anderson, the commander of Federal troops at Fort Sumter, South Carolina. Situated on a small island in the middle of Charleston's harbor, the fort was surrounded by ships and shore batteries of the newly formed Confederate States of America. Anderson informed the president that the garrison had only six weeks of provisions left. Would the Federal government order a withdrawal or resupply the outpost? This was quite a dilemma, as resupplying the fort might trigger a military response from the Confederates. Surrendering the fort was not an option, as Lincoln had promised in his inaugural speech to "hold, occupy and possess" all Federal property.

At a meeting of his cabinet on March 9, President Lincoln asked that they present him with their opinions on the matter in one week. When they reported back to him, their recommendations varied and no consensus was reached. Lincoln realized that the consequential decision was his alone to make and that time was running short. On March 29, he ordered the navy to send ships to resupply the fortress. When the Confederates learned of this plan they called upon Major Anderson to surrender. Upon his refusal to do so, the Confederate guns opened fire on Fort Sumter at 4:30 a.m. on April 12, 1861. The Civil War had begun. The 127 man force under Anderson's command returned fire. After suffering 33 hours of bombardment, against overwhelming odds, they finally surrendered. Following this, the defenders of the fort were permitted to board a ship and return to the north.

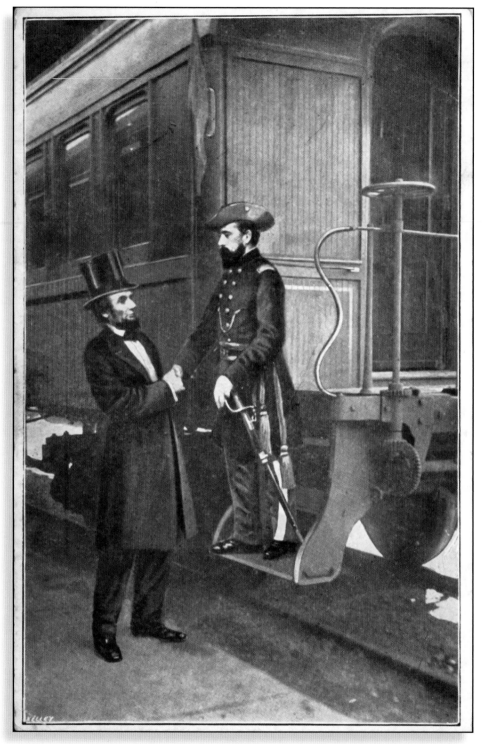

When the war began on April 12, with the firing on Fort Sumter, the city of Washington was virtually defenseless. It wasn't until April 19 that the first Union soldiers, the 6th Massachusetts Regiment, entered the capital. President Lincoln welcomed Colonel Edward F. Jones, the unit's commander, and his troops when they arrived by train from Baltimore. While passing through Baltimore the regiment suffered four dead and many wounded when they were attacked by an angry mob of secessionists.
c. 1900, Defenders of the Flag, Binghamton, NY [$20-25]

Three days after the firing on Fort Sumter, President Lincoln called for 75,000 volunteers to join the Federal cause. Several days later he then ordered the navy to begin a blockade of the southern ports to prevent their trade with foreign nations. The northern free-states rallied behind the president. At this point four more southern slave states seceded and joined the Confederacy. To help suppress violence and crush rebellion in territory under his control, Lincoln suspended the writ of habeas corpus. This allowed the military to arrest anyone without the necessity of showing just cause. Chief Justice Roger B. Taney of the Supreme Court ruled that this was unwarranted and many felt that Lincoln was assuming tyrannical powers. Nevertheless the army continued to disregard these opinions for most of the war.

The first real battle of the war took place just about 20 miles southwest of Washington near Manassas, Virginia. On a hot Sunday, July 21, 1861, Union troops under General Irvin McDowell engaged the Confederates led by General Beauregard and General Joseph E. Johnston. Much of the fighting took place near a small creek named Bull Run. Nearly 35,000 Union soldiers, many of them relatively new recruits, were successful at first. Late in the afternoon, Confederate reinforcements arrived allowing for a counter attack. The Union lines broke and the soldiers ran. It became a clear victory for the Confederates. With this defeat, at what became known as the 1st Battle of Bull Run, the North realized that it was going to be a long war. This realization may have led Lincoln to impose the first Federal income tax in August, 1861.

Hoping to find a commander who might turn things around, Lincoln replaced General McDowell (who had taken over from the old and infirm General Winfield Scott), with General George B. McClellan, just six days after the debacle at Bull Run. McClellan took note of the fact that the army suffered from a lack of training and he set about to transform the troops into a fighting force.

Before taking command of the Union Army, McClellan was a strong advocate for offensive action. This was one of the things that Lincoln had liked about him. Once in charge however, McClellan hesitated and kept postponing major actions against the enemy. It seemed to Lincoln that he always had excuses for not taking the fight more vigorously to the South. By winter, the Army of the Potomac still had not engaged in any substantial campaigns.

Good news arrived from the west in early February of 1862. Federal forces under the command of General Ulysses S. Grant captured Fort Henry and Fort Donelson in Tennessee. These first Union victories gave some hope to the president.

Early in January, 1862, Lincoln replaced his Secretary of War, Simon Cameron, with Edwin M. Stanton. Before this, Stanton had been a strong critic of Lincoln and his policies. But his strengths as an organizer helped bring order to the War Department. His efficiency also helped to curtail the waste and fraud that had marked Cameron's tenure. Stanton would become a powerful asset for the president.

Personal tragedy struck the Lincoln family again on February 20, 1862. Willie Lincoln, who had fallen ill with what was probably typhoid fever, died at the age of 12. With the death of their second son, both Abe and Mary were overcome with intense grief. Mary, especially, took the death hard and would display bouts of uncontrollable screaming and moaning. She dressed herself all in black as a sign of mourning. It would be two years before she returned to normal attire. Mary spoke of seeing the ghost of Willie at the foot of her bed and she tried to contact him through the use of spiritual mediums. Abe had the body of his beloved son exhumed on two occasions, just so that he might gaze upon his face again. At last the president was able to come to terms with his loss and put the devastating bereavement behind him. He went back to dedicating himself to the running of the nation.

Between May 6 and May 11, 1862, Lincoln visited Fort Monroe in Virginia. There he met with General John E. Wool and personally helped plan the attack on Norfolk. Norfolk was successfully captured and the Confederates forced to blow up the ironclad *Merrimack* to prevent its seizure.
Walter H. Miller, Williamsburg, VA [$2-4]

Finally, in the spring of 1862, the Union Army of the Potomac began to move. On March 10 McClellan's forces left their camps around Washington and advanced on to the Manassas area. The Confederates anticipating these movements abandoned their fortifications and withdrew. In response, McClellan moved his army by boat to the lower Chesapeake region, landing at Fortress Monroe on April 1. From there he marched on Richmond, moving slowly and often complaining about his lack of sufficient numbers of troops. As he approached Yorktown, the Confederates evacuated. After this, Lincoln traveled to Fortress Monroe to discuss the campaign with McClellan. The general believed that he was greatly outnumbered and argued that he needed more soldiers. Ultimately Lincoln would not send him more, citing a vital need to have adequate forces with which to defend the capital. By May 26 the Union Army was within five miles of Richmond. The Confederates, under General Joseph E. Johnston, attacked the Federals. Johnston was severely wounded in the action, resulting in Jefferson Davis replacing him with Robert E. Lee. Lee continued offensive actions and after a series of engagements referred to as the Seven Days battles, drove McClellan back to Washington. McClellan complained that it was the lack of reinforcements that led to his defeat and that the president was to blame.

Meanwhile, in early April, Union forces in the west defeated the Confederates at the Battle of Shiloh. The cost of this victory was high, with 13,000 dead and wounded. This was followed by the successful capture of New Orleans by Admiral David Farragut and his naval forces on April 25. Not satisfied with McClellan's performance Lincoln replaced him as general-in-chief with General Henry W. Halleck on July 11, 1862. In the course of the war Lincoln would dismiss and assign a succession of commanders to head his armies. After Generals Scott, McDowell, McClellan, and Halleck the Generals Burnside, Hooker, Meade, and finally Grant would all have their turns at leading the army.

PRESIDENT ABRAHAM LINCOLN IN CAMP AT ANTIETAM.

On October 2, 1862 Lincoln traveled to Antietam, Maryland, to confer with General McClellan. Several photographs taken by Alexander Gardner on October 3 documented this meeting. Here Lincoln is seen with General McClellan and his staff. Included among those in this photograph is a young captain who would later become quite famous, George Armstrong Custer.
1907, Jamestown Amusement & Vending Co., Norfolk, VA [$10-12]

THE MEDIATOR
October 8, 1862

Lincoln reviews the troops while visiting Antietam. Discouraged by McClellan's cautiousness in pursuing the enemy, the president showed his displeasure by remarking, "this is General McClellan's bodyguard."
Walter H. Miller & Co., Williamsburg, VA [$2-4]

In this photograph, taken on October 3, 1862 at Antietam, Lincoln poses with the detective Allan Pinkerton and Major General John A. McClernand.
c. 1935, J.T. Richards, Bull Run, VA [$5-7]

Another great battle was to be fought on September 17. In this, the Battle of Antietam, Union troops under McClellan faced Robert E. Lee again. Here they forced Lee to retreat in what was the bloodiest single day's fighting of the war. Over 22 thousand casualties were suffered between the two sides. But just as in the past, McClellan was cautious and did not pursue his enemy. If he had, some historians believe, the war might possibly have been ended. In early October, Lincoln visited McClellan at Antietam. The president would say of his general's inaction, "he's got the slows." Before the year was over the Union Army would suffer yet another major defeat. This time the Army of the Potomac, now under command of General Burnside, was defeated at the Battle of Fredericksburg on December 13.

ABRAHAM LINCOLN

UNVEILED AT CAPITOL, WASHINGTON, D. C. ON MARCH 9, 1959, PAINTED BY JES SCHLAIKJER. SHOWS LINCOLN SITTING BESIDE HIS BED MAKING AN EARLY DRAFT OF THE EMANCIPATION PROCLAMATION.

1809 • LINCOLN SESQUICENTENNIAL • 1959

Sitting by his bedside, Lincoln works on writing what would become one of the most significant documents of his administration, the Emancipation Proclamation.
1959, W.M. Grandy, Warner, NH [$4-6]

Titled *First Reading of Emancipation Proclamation Before the Cabinet*, this painting by artist Francis B. Carpenter depicts Lincoln presenting the preliminary draft of this important document to his cabinet on September 22, 1862. The original of this painting hangs in the Capitol Building in Washington, D.C.
c. 1910, A.C. Bosselman & Co., New York, NY [$4-6]

On January 1, 1863, President Lincoln put his signature to the final draft of the Emancipation Proclamation. After signing he said, "If my name ever gets into history it will be for this act."
© 1908, H.M. Rose Co., Philadelphia, PA [$6-8]

When the Emancipation Proclamation went into effect on January 1, 1863, it freed only those slaves found within the rebelling states of the Confederacy. It wasn't until the passage of the 13th Amendment that slavery was abolished throughout the United States.
© 1908, E. Nash, New York, NY [$10-12]

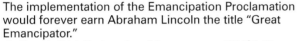

The implementation of the Emancipation Proclamation would forever earn Abraham Lincoln the title "Great Emancipator."
Authentic Distributors Inc, Massapequa, NY [$4-6]

With the victory at Antietam, Lincoln was given the opportunity that he had been waiting for. It was something he had been determined to do, but needed just the right moment in which to act. On September 22, 1862 he issued the Emancipation Proclamation. The document declared that on January 1, 1863, "all persons held as slaves within any State or designated part of a State, the people whereof shall then be in rebellion against the United States, shall be then, thenceforward, and forever FREE." This was a most meaningful document. Not satisfied with just this measure, Lincoln later went on to call for an amendment to the constitution to "terminate and forever prohibit slavery." After passing both houses of Congress, this, the 13th Amendment, was finally approved and ratified by the states on December 18, 1865. Slavery would then forever be abolished in the United States.

1863 would see more intense fighting between North and South. In May, the army, now under command of General Hooker, was defeated at Chancellorsville, Virginia. In June, Robert E. Lee, hoping to bring the war to the North, invaded southern Pennsylvania. General George Meade, who had just replaced Hooker, was with the Army of the Potomac in Maryland. Marching his forces northward, Meade and the Union Army met the Army of Northern Virginia at the small town of Gettysburg. More than 172,000 soldiers battled over 25 square miles of terrain. During July 1, 2, and 3, the largest and bloodiest battle ever to be fought on American soil took place. It would prove to be the "high water mark" of the Confederacy. The Battle of Gettysburg marked the turning point of the war. After his defeat, Lee retreated back to Virginia. Meade, like McClellan before him, failed to follow up on his victory. Allowing the crippled Army of Virginia to escape only prolonged the war for another two years of bloody fighting. The day after the victory at Gettysburg, more good news reached President Lincoln back in Washington. On July 4, Grant had captured the Confederate stronghold at Vicksburg.

Old Historic "Hanover" York County, Pennsylvania
13 MILES E. OF GETTYSBURG; 18 S. W. OF YORK; 4 E. OF LINCOLN HIGHWAY; 5 N. OF MASON AND DIXON LINE   MET. POPULATION 15000

BATTLE OF HANOVER, (PA.) JUNE 30, 1863
KILPATRICK   CUSTER   FARNSWORTH   VS.   JEB. STUART   WADE HAMPTON   FITZHUGH LEE
First Battle on "Free Soil" of the Only Two Battles Fought North of Mason & Dixon Line During Rebellion
LOSSES— UNION: 200 Killed, Wounded, Captured.   CONFEDERATE: 100 Killed-W'd-Captured. Battle Flag
PA. CIVIL WAR BATTLE MONUMENT, CENTER SQUARE. "THE CAVALRY PICKET" (DALLIN) AT COST OF $10,000-1904

HANOVER HEARS LINCOLN NOV. 18, 1863
HANOVER ONLY TOWN IN WHICH HE DELIVERED AN ADDRESS DURING WAR
"He was then on his way to Gettysburg to take part in the Consecration Services originated by the State of Pennsylvania for the purpose of paying a tribute to the dead soldiers who had given up their lives for their country in the battle which took place in and around that borough July 1, 2, and 3, 1863, when the Confederate forces under Lee were defeated by Meade and driven back to Virginia. Lincoln had spent the time between Hanover Junction and Hanover in revising his speech to be delivered the next day at Gettysburg. He sat in a seat alone while on this trip. Shortly before the train pulled out Rev. M. J. Alleman, Pastor of St. Matthews Lutheran Church called out in loud tones: "Father Abraham, your children want to see you. Will you come to the rear platform of the car?" A minute later the tall form of Abraham Lincoln passed out of the door of the rear car. He was six feet, three inches high, and as he wore a high silk hat, Lincoln was compelled to remove it before he could appear on the platform. The words recalled by persons who were witnesses to this incident was the fact that Lincoln referred to the cavalry engagement which had taken place in and around Hanover June 30, 1863, the day before the battle of Gettysburg opened. With unbared head Lincoln said in amusing tones: "I trust when the enemy was here the citizens of Hanover were loyal to Our Country and the Stars and Stripes." Meantime the train pulled out and the presidential party moved toward Gettysburg where Lincoln immortalized himself in a four minute address.   3

On November 18, 1863, while on his way to Gettysburg, Lincoln's train paused in the town of Hanover, Pennsylvania. Shortly before pulling out of the station he spoke a few words to gathered town folk from the rear platform of his train car.
1939, William Anthony, Hanover, PA [$5-7]

The Lincoln Room

After arriving in Gettysburg on November 18, 1863, Lincoln spent the night at the home of David Wills. It was Wills who had invited the president to come and take part in the dedication ceremonies of the new National Cemetery. In his bedroom that night, Lincoln put the finishing touches on his speech.
L.E. Smith, Gettysburg, PA [$2-4]

CHICAGO HISTORICAL SOCIETY

GETTYSBURG ADDRESS, 1863

Following a two hour speech given by famed orator Edward Everett, Lincoln rose to deliver his address. The crowd quietly awaited the president's remarks.
1944, Chicago Historical Society, Chicago, IL [$4-6]

After the Battle of Gettysburg the governor of Pennsylvania appointed David Wills, a local attorney, to begin the establishment of a cemetery in which to inter the bodies of those who fell in battle. It was to be the first cemetery exclusively for the burial of military dead. Seventeen acres of ground was selected and the interment of the dead began. A ceremony was planned to take place on November 19, 1863, to dedicate this new burial ground. Wills invited the president to come and participate. Lincoln arrived the day before and spent the night at the Wills house where he put the finishing touches on his speech. At the dedication ceremonies the next day, the president was scheduled to speak after the famed orator, Edward Everett. Following a two hour speech by Everett, Lincoln rose to render his remarks to the 15,000 people who had gathered to hear him. His words took just over two minutes to deliver. Afterward Lincoln was disappointed with his presentation and felt it to be inadequate. History however would prove otherwise. This speech, the Gettysburg Address, is considered to be one of the finest in our nation's history.

LINCOLN'S ADDRESS AT GETTYSBURG.

"Four score and seven years ago, our fathers brought forth upon this continent, a new nation, conceived in liberty, and dedicated to the proposition that all men are created equal." With these words Lincoln began his famous address.
c. 1910, Raphael Tuck & Sons, London, England [$8-10]

LINCOLN DELIVERING HIS FAMOUS ADDRESS AT THE DEDICATION OF GETTYSBURG CEMETERY, NOV. 19, 1863.

It took Lincoln only a little over two minutes to deliver his Gettysburg Address, which consisted of only 10 sentences. Those carefully crafted words would be embraced forever.
© *1908, W.M. Taggart, New York, NY [$12-15]*

President Lincoln first met General Ulysses S. Grant face to face on March 8, 1864. The next day Grant was promoted to lieutenant general and became commander of all the Union armies.
c. 1910, Raphael Tuck & Sons, London, England [$8-10]

Meeting of President LINCOLN and Gen'l GRANT.

When 1864 arrived, the president could look back to the previous year with some satisfaction. Despite some losses, the Union Army had finally scored some major victories. He wanted to maintain the pressure on the rebellious states and try to destroy their military capabilities. To do this he needed a commander who was tenacious, daring, and not afraid to fight. Lincoln believed he finally had just the man for the job. On March 9, 1864 in the presence of his cabinet, Lincoln promoted Ulysses S. Grant to the rank of lieutenant general. This was a rank held previously only by George Washington. The next day Grant was given overall command of all the Union armies. Grant then developed a plan by which Union forces would put continual pressure on the Army of Northern Virginia. He then ordered General Meade, who still commanded the Army of the Potomac, to go on the offensive, stating "wherever Lee goes, there you will go also."

Early in May, nearly 100,000 Union soldiers marched across the Rapidan River in Virginia and entered an area known as the Wilderness. There they engaged the Confederate Army in many days of intense fighting. Despite heavy losses, Grant did not withdraw, as his predecessors would have. Instead he maintained contact with the enemy. In the first month alone he lost 60,000 men in combat. He would keep up these tactics until the spring of 1865, trying to keep the Confederates on the defensive. Further to the south another tactic was employed, as General William Tecumseh Sherman pushed his way through Georgia. On September 2, Atlanta fell to his troops, another major blow to the Confederacy. Not stopping here, Sherman continued onwards, leaving a path of destruction behind him as he marched to the sea. Just five days before Christmas he reached Savannah, Georgia. On December 22, Sherman victoriously telegraphed the president with the message, "I beg to present to you as a Christmas gift the city of Savannah."

On July 12, 1864, while Confederate troops under General Jubal A. Early were menacing the outskirts of the capital, Lincoln visited Fort Stevens. While there he came under direct fire from enemy sharpshooters. A medical officer standing by his side was killed.
c. 1930, Publisher unknown [$6-8]

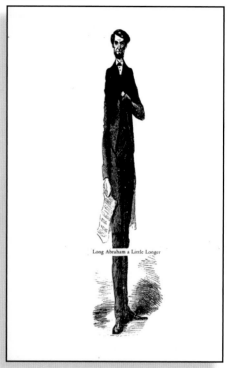

Shortly after his re-election to a second term as president, this political cartoon of Lincoln, drawn by Frank Bellew, appeared in *Harper's Weekly*.
Authentic Distributors Inc., Massapequa, NY [$4-6]

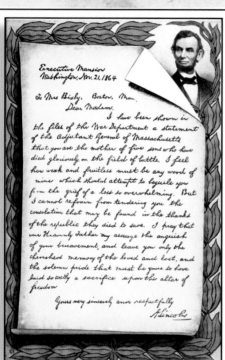

After being told of a widow named Mrs. Lydia Bixby who had lost five sons in the war, Lincoln responded with a letter. Writing to her on November 21, 1864, he expressed his great sympathy over her sacrifice. This letter was later published in a Boston newspaper and widely read. However, the president had been misinformed. Only two sons had been killed in combat, while two had deserted and one honorably discharged from service.
© 1910, M.T. Sheahan, Boston, MA [$4-6]

While the gears of war were grinding up the lives of thousands of soldiers, the political wars continued as well. At the National Union Convention held in Baltimore, June 7, 1864, members of the Republican Party and "pro Union" Democrats nominated Abraham Lincoln for re-election. His running mate was Andrew Johnson of Tennessee. The Democratic Party nominated none other than George McClellan, Lincoln's former army commander. McClellan ran on a platform stating that, if elected, he would permit slavery and bring about peace "at the earliest possible moment." When Election Day came on November 8, Lincoln and Johnson received 55% of the popular vote and 212 of 233 possible electoral votes. The president now looked forward to serving four more years, with hopes of reuniting the nation.

On February 3, 1865 Lincoln traveled on the steamboat *River Queen* down to Hampton Roads, Virginia. There he met with a delegation of officials from the Confederate States of America and discussed the possibility of peace. Unfortunately the talks failed and he returned to Washington. In the meantime, Union forces were continually doing battle with the Confederate Army on several fronts, drawing the noose tighter. Sherman had captured Charleston, South Carolina, on February 7, and marched north into North Carolina and Virginia. Grant was still laying siege to Petersburg and threatening Richmond. Lincoln was looking for ways to bring the long war to an end.

After taking the oath of office, Lincoln delivered his Second Inaugural Address before a large crowd. In his speech, considered one of his finest, he called upon the nation to "bind up its wounds" and to go forth with "malice towards none; and charity for all."
© *1908, E. Nash, New York, NY [$10-12]*

This photograph taken March 4, 1865, shows Lincoln delivering his Second Inaugural Address. On the railed balcony behind him stands the man who would later be his assassin, John Wilkes Booth. Some historians believe that several of Booth's fellow conspirators can be seen positioned just below the speaker's podium.
c. 1910, K-win & Co., Chicago, IL [$12-15]

March 4 was the day for the president's second inauguration. It was an overcast, threatening day as Chief Justice Salmon P. Chase prepared to administer the oath of office. But, as Lincoln stepped forward, the clouds parted and the sun broke through. Chase would comment later that it was "an auspicious omen … of the clear sunlight of prosperous peace." Addressing the people gathered in front of the Capitol, Lincoln spoke of a need for the nation to heal and to seek a lasting peace. The nation should be one "with malice toward none; with charity for all."

JOHN WILKES BOOTH
ASSASSINATED PRESIDENT LINCOLN, APRIL 14, 1865

A photographic portrait of John Wilkes Booth, the assassin of President Lincoln. At 26 years of age, he was one of the most famous actors of his day and a renowned ladies' man. A supporter of the Southern cause, he had developed an intense hatred for the North and of Abraham Lincoln in particular. After his initial plots to kidnap the president had failed, he decided to take more drastic measures.
© 1907, Buckingham & Harley, Washington, D.C. [$15-20]

THE ASSASSINS OF PRESIDENT LINCOLN

John Wilkes Booth shown with his band of accomplices. These are the individuals that Booth conspired with to kidnap the president, and later involved in the assassination plot.
© 1907, Buckingham & Harley, Washington, D.C. [$15-20]

As he gave his short speech there were those in the audience watching and listening who had other things on their mind. Among the spectators was John Wilkes Booth and several of his associates. Booth was plotting to kidnap the president on March 17, while he was on his way to visit the Soldiers Home. During his presidency, Lincoln had often ridden out to the Soldiers Home, only three miles north of the White House. It was a place where he spent much of his time, and it often served as a summer refuge for the Lincoln family. Booth hoped to capture the president and smuggle him away to the South. There it was hoped, he could be ransomed for the release of Confederate soldiers, who could then continue the war. Despite his plans, the plot failed when Lincoln did not show as expected.

13361.   Soldiers' Home, Washington, D. C.

Located just a few miles north of the White House, the Soldier's Home was established in 1851. The 14-room house known as Anderson Cottage, seen just to the left of the main building, served as the summer retreat for several presidents. Lincoln spent almost 30% of his presidency here during the years 1862-1864. It was here that he first worked on the writing of the Emancipation Proclamation.
c. 1912, I. & M. Ottenheimer, Baltimore, MD [$4-6]

MRS. MARY SURRATT'S HOUSE
WHERE THE CONSPIRATORS HELD THEIR MEETINGS

The Surratt Boardinghouse, a three-story brick home at 541 K Street, was only a few blocks from Ford's Theatre. Mary Surratt, whose son John was a Confederate agent, ran the house. A safe haven for Confederate spies and couriers, it was here that Booth and his fellow conspirators plotted the kidnapping of the president.
© 1907, Buckingham & Harley, Washington, D.C. [$15-18]

Lincoln traveled to City Point, Virginia on March 24, 1865. He stayed there for two weeks conferring with General Grant and others about war plans. He toured City Point, which was the main supply depot supporting the siege of Petersburg, and even visited the front lines.
Arthur Jaffe Heliochrome Co., New York, NY [$4-6]

April 4, 1865, just two days after the fall of Petersburg and the evacuation of Richmond that followed, Lincoln entered the former Confederate capital. Accompanied by his son Tad and a small detachment of sailors, the president walked the streets of Richmond.
c. 1908, International Art Publishing Co., New York, NY [$8-10]

"WITH·MALICE·TOWARDS·NONE;·WITH·CHARITY·FOR·ALL".
President Lincoln's entry into Richmond.
· April 4th, 1865 ·

While delivering his inaugural, Lincoln knew that the conclusion of the war was approaching. Near the end of March, Lincoln once again boarded the steamer *River Queen* and sailed to Virginia. At Grant's headquarters at City Point, the president met with Grant, General Sherman, and Admiral Porter. They discussed plans for the end of the war. While still at City Point, Lincoln received word that Petersburg, after 10 months of siege, had fallen on April 2. The Confederate government ordered the evacuation of Richmond and set fire to public and government buildings. The flames spread and destroyed some 700 structures in a single day. The Confederacy was now in its death throes. On April 4, Lincoln entered the city of Richmond, the former capital of the Confederacy. Escorted by only a small military detachment, he walked through the streets and was greeted by welcoming crowds of former, now freed, slaves.

The president returned to Washington aboard the *River Queen*, arriving on April 9, 1865. Upon his arrival he learned that General Robert E. Lee, surrounded and with his army threatened with annihilation, had surrendered. It was at the private home of Wilmer McLean that Lee met with Grant to discuss the surrender terms. Ironically, McLean had

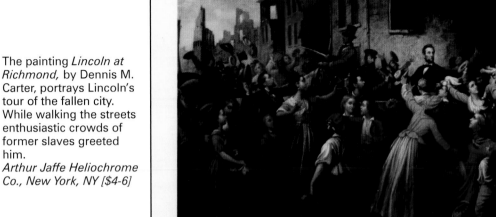

The painting *Lincoln at Richmond,* by Dennis M. Carter, portrays Lincoln's tour of the fallen city. While walking the streets enthusiastic crowds of former slaves greeted him.
Arthur Jaffe Heliochrome Co., New York, NY [$4-6]

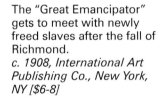

The "Great Emancipator" gets to meet with newly freed slaves after the fall of Richmond.
c. 1908, International Art Publishing Co., New York, NY [$6-8]

previously lived in Manassas where his home was located at the site of the first battle. To escape the war he had moved to the quiet small town of Appomattox Court House, only to have the war ended in his parlor. The Army of Northern Virginia was no more. Essentially the great Civil War was finished. All that remained was for some of the smaller units of the Confederate Army to surrender as well, which they did in short order.

Cities and towns across the North rejoiced upon hearing the news that the great, bloody conflict was now over. In Washington, like other cities, church bells rang, cannons were fired, and flags and bunting seemed to decorate every building. It was a time of great celebration. On April 10 cheering crowds gathered on the lawn of the White House. Lincoln appeared before them and gave a brief oration at the conclusion of which he said "I have always thought "Dixie" one of the best tunes I have ever heard. Our adversaries over the way attempted to appropriate it, but I insisted yesterday that we fairly captured it…I now request the band to favor me with its performance." The great burden of the war had been lifted from his shoulders. The problems of reconstruction and the reuniting of the nation remained. But Abraham Lincoln would never live to see this accomplished.

Chapter 4

Assassination &
the Journey Home
(1865)

Dawn broke on the morning of April 14, 1865 and it appeared that it would be a splendid day in Washington, D.C. It was Good Friday. Just the day before, General Grant had returned fresh from Appomattox Court House and had been greeted by exuberant crowds. The city was still in a festive mood since the word of Lee's surrender had reached the people less than a week before. The president awoke early and went to his office to handle a few matters. At about 8:00 he had breakfast with Mary and their two sons. Robert, age 21, was a captain serving on Grant's staff. Having just returned from the scene of Lee's surrender he told his mother and father about life at the front and described the surrender itself. He then gave his father a small portrait of Robert E. Lee. After studying the picture for awhile the president made the comment, "It is a good face, I am glad the war is over at last."

Back in his office again by 9:00, the president received visitors. The day was shaping up to be a very busy one, much the same as many before it. People came to congratulate him on the success of the war, congressmen came on political business, and others for favors. He made several minor appointments and even signed a number of pardons, which was much easier to do now that the war was over. At 11:00 the cabinet met, with General Grant in attendance, to discuss Reconstruction. While this was taking place a very symbolic ceremony was being held in Charleston, South Carolina. Major General Robert Anderson had returned to once again raise the Stars and Stripes over Fort Sumter. Exactly four years before, on April 14, 1861, Anderson had lowered this very same flag before departing the surrendered fortress. It was an emotional ceremony, followed up by the celebratory firing of cannon from the Federal fleet and land artillery.

Lincoln's Last Official Act
Published by Gutekunst, Boston

Just hours before his assassination, President Lincoln signed several pardons. One of these was an application for a discharge, upon the taking of an oath of allegiance, for a Confederate prisoner. He signed the petition with the words, "Let it be done."
c. 1950s, Publisher unknown [$4-6]

At what would be Lincoln's last cabinet meeting he told the members assembled about a prophetic dream he had recently. At various times in his life he had dreams, which he said had always foretold some future event of significance. In regards to this dream, he described how he saw himself in "some indescribable vessel and I was moving with great rapidity toward an indefinite shore." He believed this was a portent of something important, but he knew not what. The meeting continued until about 2:00, at which time the president went to have lunch with his wife. After that it was back to the office to see more visitors and to attend to more business.

Late in the afternoon the president and Mary Lincoln took a carriage ride together out to the Navy Yard to view several war ships that had been damaged in a naval engagement at Fort Fisher, North Carolina. Mary said of her husband, " I never saw him so supremely cheerful." On their ride they talked about what life would be like when they returned home to Springfield. Lincoln spoke of his wishes that "we may hope for four years of peace and happiness, and then we will go back to Illinois and pass the rest of our lives in quiet." They arrived back at the White House in time to have a family dinner with their sons. Afterwards the president walked over to the War Department, as he had so often done before, to see if any word had come from General Sherman regarding the expected surrender of General Johnston and his army. No messages had arrived so he returned to the Executive Mansion.

Like others around him, as the president was going through the routine of his day, he was unaware that a group of conspirators was plotting his assassination. The leader of this group was the famed actor John Wilkes Booth. Booth had strong sympathies for the Southern cause and had a growing hatred for the North and particularly towards President Lincoln. Back on July 26, 1864, while in Boston, he had been recruited to help the Confederate Secret Service. One of Booth's earlier plans had been to kidnap the president. When that had failed he decided to take more extreme measures. When the chance arose, Booth planned to murder Abraham Lincoln, the man he blamed for all of the South's problems.

On the morning of April 14, while at Ford's Theatre, Booth learned that the president would be attending that evening's performance of the comedy play *Our American Cousin*. His opportunity to strike on familiar ground had come. With this information he left and began to put his plans into motion. Late in the afternoon he returned to the theater and made his preparations. This included carving a peephole in the door to the presidential box, and the making of a wooden door jam to bar the door to the box behind him once he entered. When all was in order he left the building. A little after 8:00 p.m., Booth met with his partners in crime for the last time in room six of the Herndon House, a boarding house close to Ford's Theatre. Assignments, final instructions, and the details of that evening's plans were discussed. George Atzerodt was assigned to kill the vice president, while Lewis Powell (alias Paine) was to gain entrance to the home of the Secretary of State, William Seward, and assassinate him. David Herold was to assist Powell in his escape. Everything was now set, all they needed to do was carry out their intentions.

Located at 511 10th Street, the Ford's Theatre building was originally a Baptist Church. Converted into a music hall in 1861, it was damaged by fire, rebuilt, and opened as Ford's New Theatre in 1863. Today it is in restored condition and a National Historic Site.
c. 1910, A.C. Bosselman & Co., New York, NY [$2-4]

Lincoln attended at least 12 performances here, including one in 1863 in which John Wilkes Booth had the starring role. Immediately after the assassination, the owner, John Ford, was imprisoned for more than one month until he was cleared of any involvement in the murder.
Washington Novelty Co., Washington, D.C.

While the assassins were finalizing their plans, the Lincolns were just leaving the White House. Earlier in the day, Mary Lincoln had made the arrangements to attend Ford's Theatre that evening. Originally it was planned that the Grants would accompany them. However, the Grants canceled the invitation later in the day. In all, 14 people would decline the offer to go with them that night. At last arrangements were made to go with Major Henry Rathbone and his fiancee Clara Harris. After picking up their last minute guests, the carriage delivered the couples to the theater at about 8:30. The president and his party entered and they were shown to the presidential box.

Already in progress, the play was halted, and the people in the audience rose to their feet cheering and applauding. The orchestra played the familiar "Hail to the Chief." Once the Lincolns were seated the play resumed. To those in the audience who looked up, it appeared that the president was enjoying the performance.

A scene done in miniature of how the stage in Ford's Theatre looked on the night of Abraham Lincoln's assassination. On the right is the presidential box.
c. 1950s, Publisher unknown [$4-6]

PRIVATE BOX
IN WHICH PRESIDENT LINCOLN WAS ASSASSINATED

This photograph shows the private presidential box occupied on the evening of April 14, 1865, by President Lincoln, his wife Mary, Major Henry Rathbone and his fiancee Clara Harris. The Treasury flag at the right front corner of the box is the one in which Booth caught his spur while leaping to the stage below.
© 1907, Buckingham & Harley, Washington, D.C. [$15-20]

The Star Saloon, owned by Peter Taltaval, was frequented by the actors and patrons of Ford's Theatre next door. Here around 10:00 p.m. that fateful night, Booth had a final drink to bolster his courage before entering the theater to commit his murderous act.
William H. Miller & Co., Williamsburg, VA [$2-4]

Abraham Lincoln was assassinated while attending a performance of the play *Our American Cousin* at Ford's Theatre. It was Good Friday, April 14, 1865. This postcard misprinted the date of his death as being in December rather than April.
© *1909, Philip Sander, New York, NY [$12-15]*

There were two doors leading into the presidential box. Having made preparations earlier in the day for his assassination attempt, John Wilkes Booth entered through the unguarded outer door unnoticed. Barring the door behind himself, he quietly opened the inner door to reveal his target.
National Historical Wax Museum, Washington, D.C. [$2-4]

When the play was in its third act Booth entered the theater. The president's bodyguard, policeman John F. Parker, had left his post to get a better seat from which to watch the play. The White House coachman, who had also been seated near the box, had done the same. Booth was able to approach the president's box unchallenged. Without making a sound, Booth opened the outer door and walked inside. He then barred the door behind him with the piece of wood he had placed there earlier in the day. Glancing through the peephole he had made, he saw that the president was sitting in a high-backed rocking chair near the rear of the box. Booth then stepped quietly and unnoticed through the inner door. He drew his weapons. With him he had a single shot derringer and a large hunting knife. Below on the stage, the actor Harry Hawk was delivering this line, "Wal, I guess I know enough to turn you inside out, old gal – you sockdologizing, old mantrap." These would be the last words that Lincoln would ever hear. At that moment, perhaps sensing something behind him, Lincoln apparently turned his head slightly to his left. Booth then stepped directly behind the president, placed his small pistol to the back of his victim's head, and pulled the trigger. The bullet struck just behind the left ear and penetrated Lincoln's brain, coming to rest just behind the right eye. It was about 10:13 p.m.

While the president's attention was on the play being acted out below him, Booth approached with gun in hand. Placing the small derringer to the back of Lincoln's head, Booth pulled the trigger.
Grant-Mann Lithographers, Vancouver, Canada [$2-4]

The assassination scene as it was depicted on the front page of *Leslie's Illustrated Newspaper* published on April 29, 1865.
c. 1950s, Publisher unknown [$4-6]

It was this .44 caliber, single shot derringer with black walnut stock, that was used by John Wilkes Booth to shoot the president. This weapon is now on display at the Ford's Theatre Museum.
Parks and History Assoc., Washington, D.C. [$2-4]

Lincoln's Death Chair, Greenfield Village

The black walnut rocking chair, upholstered in red damask, in which Lincoln was sitting when shot by Booth. Henry Ford purchased the chair at an auction in New York City in 1929 for $2,400. It is now on display at Greenfield Village in Dearborn, Michigan.
1958, Curteich, Chicago, IL [$3-5]

Booth, having shot the president, leapt to the stage below. Catching his spur in the Treasury flag decorating the box, he landed off balance breaking his leg. Standing, he shouted "sic semper tyrannis!" before rushing off stage and making his escape.
1908, M.W. Taggart, New York, NY [$12-15]

ASSASSINATION OF
PRESIDENT LINCOLN
APRIL 14, 1865.

FORD'S THEATRE DRAPED IN MOURNING

The president slumped forward fatally wounded. At the sound of the shot, Major Rathbone jumped from his seat and tried to grab the assailant. Booth slashed deeply into Rathbone's upper arm with his knife. As some in the audience glanced upwards, Booth jumped over the balcony to the stage some 12 feet below. In doing so, one of his spurs caught in a flag that was draped in front of the box, causing him to land off balance. A bone in his left foot, near the ankle, snapped. He then stood, and ever the actor, dramatically shouted out, "sic semper tyrannis!" (thus ever to tyrants!). While confusion mounted, Booth ran across the stage toward the back door. On his way out he slashed again with his blade, this time the orchestra leader William Withers, who stood in his path, was the target. Doing no real harm, Booth continued out into the alley where he mounted his waiting horse and rode off into the night making his escape.

Back in the theater, the shocked and terrified crowd shouted, cursed, and screamed. Some having recognized Booth as the attacker began shouting his name. Within moments two doctors gained entrance to the box and began attending to the stricken president. Doctors Charles Leale and Charles Taft quickly assessed Lincoln's wound. After administering mouth to mouth resuscitation, Dr. Leale detected a weak pulse and the victim had begun breathing on his own. Two other doctors arrived and seeing the need to move the president lifted him up and with the aid of several others carried him from the box, down the stairs, and out of the theater.

LINCOLN BORNE BY LOVING HANDS — LINCOLN MUSEUM, WASHINGTON

After being attended to by doctors on the scene, the body of Abraham Lincoln was carried across 10th Street to the Peterson Boarding House. An artist, who happened to be nearby and thus able to sketch the event as it was happening, made this painting capturing the historic moment.
1935, Welfare and Recreation Assoc., Washington, D.C. [$4-6]

The House in which Lincoln Died, Washington, D. C.

Peterson's Boarding House, 516 10th Street, was located across from Ford's Theatre. It was here that Lincoln's body was taken after he was shot. He was placed in a small, first floor room, at the back of the house.
c. 1920, W.B. Garrison, Washington, D.C. [$4-6]

By this time soldiers had cleared a passage through the crowds. Once outside, they were directed across Tenth Street to a small rooming house that was owned by William Peterson. Lincoln was placed on a bed in a small bedroom on the first floor, near the back of the building. As the bed was too short to accommodate Lincoln's height, an attempt was made to break off the foot rails. Unable to do so, it became necessary to lay the fallen president diagonally across the bed. Doctors, attempting to treat the fatal wound, attended to him throughout the night. At various times, visitors of all ranks entered the small room where they observed the president as his life slowly ebbed away. In all, more than 90 people would visit the room during that long night. Out in the street, in front of the Peterson house, a large assemblage stood vigil over their fallen leader. There was not much that the doctors could do except try to make the president as comfortable as possible. Word arrived that Secretary Seward had been attacked and severely wounded and that the attacker had escaped. Seward would survive his horrendous wounds. Later it was learned that an attempt on the life of Vice President Johnson had also been planned but never carried out.

Room in which Lincoln died
House where Lincoln died - Washington, D.C.   3-K-67

The room where Lincoln was taken measured only 10 x 15 feet. It's bed was so short that the president had to be laid diagonally across it.
c. 1950s, Publisher unknown [$4-6]

According to Gideon Welles (Secretary of the Navy), who was present at the scene, Mary Lincoln would sit by the bedside of her stricken husband "about once an hour … until overcome by emotion." Later, Edwin Stanton would bar her from the room.
Florida Natural Color Inc., Miami, FL {$2-4]

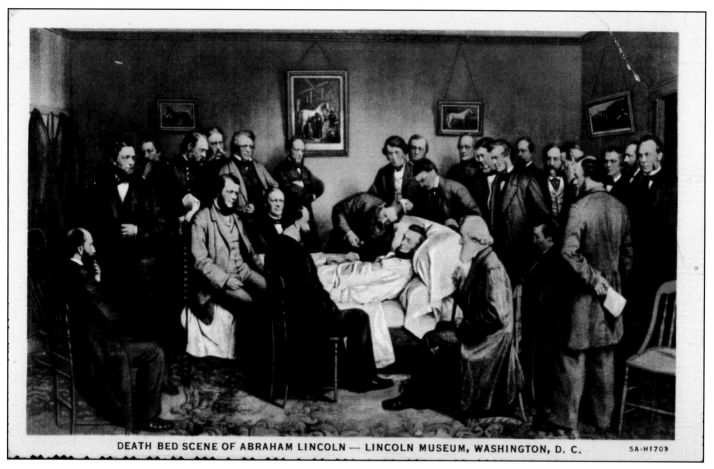

DEATH BED SCENE OF ABRAHAM LINCOLN — LINCOLN MUSEUM, WASHINGTON, D. C.   5A-H1709

Never regaining consciousness, Abraham Lincoln died surrounded by doctors and government officials, at 7:22 a.m. on April 15, 1865. As Edwin Stanton so appropriately stated, "He now belongs to
the ages."
1935, Welfare and Recreation Assoc., Washington, D.C. [$4-6]

At last dawn came. Outside it was raining, but the people still silently waited. Because she had displayed a fit of hysteria the night before, Secretary Stanton ordered
that Mary Lincoln be kept away, restricted to a room at the front of the house. Those of
importance gathered at the bedside awaiting the end. All knew that the president could
not hold on much longer. His breathing became more labored and then weakened. Doc-
tor Taft, sitting by the bed recorded that at 7:22 a.m. and 10 seconds on April 15, 1865,
the president's heart stopped beating. Abraham Lincoln was dead. The Reverend Dr.
Gurley said a brief prayer. After a short period of time, Edwin Stanton standing at the
foot of the bed with tears in his eyes, was heard to say those immortal words, "Now
he belongs to the ages."

Shortly after his death, Lincoln's body was transported back to the White House.
There an autopsy was performed in a guest room on the northeast corner of the second
floor. Afterwards the body was embalmed, dressed, and prepared for the funerals to
come. On Tuesday, April 18, lines of people began to enter the White House to view
the body. The next day, a little after 12:00 noon, funeral services were held in the East
Room of the White House, presided over by four ministers and attended by 600 guests.
Simultaneously in churches all across the country similar services were being held. It
was estimated that some 25 million people took part in these observances. After the
funeral, a great procession accompanied Lincoln's body to the Capitol. There it laid in
state for public viewing.

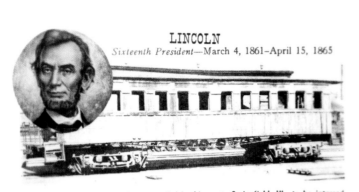

LINCOLN
Sixteenth President—March 4, 1861–April 15, 1865

The body of Abraham Lincoln was carried in this car to Springfield, Ill., to be interred. The car was built at the Military Car Shops, Alexandria, Va., in 1864. In order to make the car bullet proof armor plate was placed between the inner and outer walls. President Lincoln's study was in the largest compartment, and the long sofa in it was used as Lincoln's bed at night. The Union Pacific purchased the car in 1866, and it was exhibited at the Trans-Mississippi International Exposition at Omaha, Neb., in 1898.

This postcard shows the train car that carried the bodies of Abraham Lincoln and his son Willie back to Springfield, Illinois. Originally built as an armored car for transporting the president and his cabinet, it was hastily remodeled to serve as a funeral car.
c. 1950s, Publisher unknown [$4-6]

THE LINCOLN FUNERAL CAR
SOUVENIR
42ND NATIONAL ENCAMPMENT
G.A.R

The funeral train car and its honor guard are seen in this photograph taken in 1865. In later years the car was exhibited to the public, but was destroyed by a fire on March 18, 1911. This postcard was published in 1908 as a souvenir of the 42nd National G.A.R. Encampment held in Toledo, Ohio. A total of 300,000 were printed and distributed.
1908, Lamson Brothers, Toledo, OH [$20-25]

On April 22, 1865, the nine car funeral train arrived in Philadelphia. An open coffin viewing was held at Independence Hall, where an estimated 300,000 people gazed upon the president's body. At one time the double line of mourners stretched for a distance of three miles.
Bob Fremming, Dallas, WI [$3-5]

SQUARE 50 YEARS AGO.

MONUMENT SQUARE AND PAVILION, CLEVELAND, O.   REMAINS OF PRESIDENT LINCOLN LYING IN STATE 1865.

Around 7:00 a.m. on April 28, the funeral train pulled into Cleveland, Ohio. A hearse drawn by six white horses (seen in this postcard view) transported the body of the fallen president to an outdoor pavilion set up in Monument Square.
1915, Braun Postcard Co., Cleveland, OH [$8-10]

Early on the morning of Friday, April 25, a special nine car funeral train departed from Washington. Aboard the train were the bodies of Abraham Lincoln and his son Willie. Accompanying them were 300 dignitaries. They traveled now together, on a 1,700 mile trip that duplicated the route, only in reverse, to that taken by Lincoln in 1861. The train made stops in 10 major cities along the way, where other funeral services and viewings were held. Over one million mourners were said to have had the opportunity to glimpse his face once more. Where the train did not stop, people lined the tracks or stood on the platforms of the small train stations just to get a view of the passing "long black train." It was an outpouring of grief and sorrow like no other in our nation's history. At last on May 3 the train arrived in Springfield, Illinois. Every building was draped in black mourning cloth. Abraham Lincoln had come home.

The only outdoor viewing to be held for the president lasted 15 hours. In that time 150,000 people had the opportunity to look upon the face of Abraham Lincoln. At midnight the train continued on its journey.
Publisher unknown [$2-4]

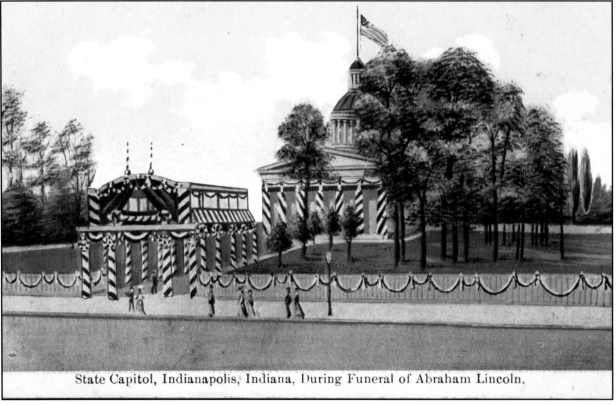

Lincoln's funeral train reached Indianapolis, Indiana, on April 30. Due to heavy rains a grand procession that had been planned was canceled. The state capitol seen here was decorated in mourning and was the site of the official viewing.
c. 1920, Publisher unknown [$12-15]

A reward poster issued by the War Department for the apprehension of those involved in the assassination was widely distributed. Eventually reward money would be divided among 34 persons.
© 1909, Philip Sander, New York, NY [$12-15]

Just 13 miles southeast of Washington, D.C., in the town of Surrattsville, Maryland (since renamed Clinton), is the combination house and tavern owned by Mary Surratt. Booth and his accomplice David Herold stopped here after the assassination. They collected guns and whiskey previously stashed here before continuing their escape to the south.
c. 1960s, Mrs. Gerry Peck, Washington, D.C. [$3-5]

While the funeral train was just beginning its journey, the intense manhunt for the assassin was coming to a close. Booth was traveling with David Herold, trying to elude capture. Herold had deserted Paine back at the Seward house the night of the assassination and had joined up with Booth when he fled Washington. After 12 days their luck would run out. In the early morning of April 26 they were finally tracked down and surrounded by soldiers on the farm of Richard Garrett, near Port Royal, Virginia. Cornered in a tobacco barn, Booth was shot in the neck by Sgt. Boston Corbett. Placed on the porch of the farmhouse, John Wilkes Booth, the assassin of Abraham Lincoln, died at 5:30 that morning. Herold was taken alive and stood trial with seven other conspirators starting on May 9. Eventually he would hang with three others. Some people believe that the conspiracy included others that were never brought to justice. There still remain a number of unanswered questions surrounding the assassination and its plot. The true answers may never be found.

SERGEANT CHARLES CORBETT
Who Shot John Wilkes Booth

Sergent Charles "Boston" Corbett, the man who claimed to have fired the shot that killed John Wilkes Booth. He would later receive a reward of $1,653.85 from the government.
© 1907, Buckingham & Harley, Washington, D.C. [$15-20]

THE HANGING OF PRESIDENT LINCOLN'S ASSASSINS

Four individuals were condemned to die for their roles in the assassination of President Lincoln and the attack on Secretary Seward. The execution took place in the prison yard of the Old Washington Penitentiary on July 7, 1865. Those hanged were Mary Surratt, Lewis Paine, David Herold, and George Atzerodt.
© 1907, Buckingham & Harley, Washington, D.C. [$15-20]

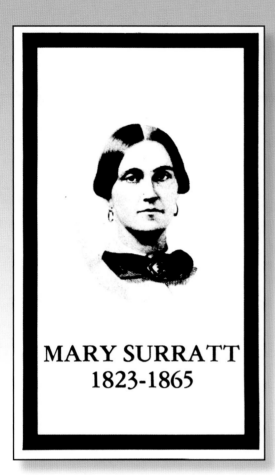

MARY SURRATT
1823-1865

Mary Surratt has the distinction of being the first woman to be executed by the United States government. At the age of 48 she was convicted and hanged as a conspirator in the assassination of President Lincoln.
Surratt Society, Clinton, MD [$2-4]

Fort Jefferson, 63 miles from Key West in the Dry Tortugas, was the prison where four of those convicted of playing a part in the assassination were sent. Those incarcerated here were Dr. Samuel Mudd, Samuel Arnold, Michael O'Laughlin, and Edward Spangler.
c. 1960s, Publisher unknown [$2-4]

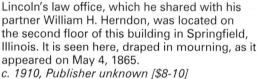

Lincoln's law office, which he shared with his partner William H. Herndon, was located on the second floor of this building in Springfield, Illinois. It is seen here, draped in mourning, as it appeared on May 4, 1865.
c. 1910, Publisher unknown [$8-10]

The home of Abraham Lincoln, with its eaves and windows draped in black bunting, is seen as it appeared on the day of the funeral. Many hundreds of people visited the house that day to pay their respects.
c. 1910, Publisher unknown [$8-10]

THE ABEND DRUM

Played at the Inauguration and at the Funeral of
ABRAHAM LINCOLN.

This old war relic was carried by Louis Abend of Zumbrota, Minn., all through the civil war and was in exactly twenty of the most severe battles. Mr. Abend marched at the head of the troops and played it at the inauguration of President Lincoln in 1865, and also beat the muffled role at the grave of that great martyr. The drum is now owned by Mrs. Julia Fredrichs of Zumbrota, a cousin of Mr. Abend.

Old Bob, Lincoln's horse, was photographed standing in front of the family home the day of the funeral. A special funeral blanket drapes his body. The Reverand Henry Brown, a black preacher who had done odd jobs for the Lincolns, stands beside him on the left. During the funeral procession it was Brown's honor to lead Old Bob directly behind the hearse.
c. 1910, Publisher unknown [$10-15]

This drum, carried by Louis Abend throughout the war, was played at the inauguration of President Lincoln in 1865 and also at his grave on the day of his funeral.
c. 1910, Publisher unknown [$6-8]

First Burial Place of Abraham Lincoln, Oak Ridge Cemetery, Springfield, Illinois

On May 4, 1865 the body of Abraham Lincoln was placed within this receiving vault, dug into the hillside, just below the site of his present day tomb.
1946, Curteich, Chicago, IL [$3-5]

At last, on May 4, 1865, the final memorial services for Abraham Lincoln were held. The only family members in attendance that day were Robert Lincoln and John Hanks. Mary was too distraught to attend any of the funeral services held for her husband. She had confined herself to her bedroom in extreme bereavement. She said of her husband's death, "I can never be reconciled to my loss, until the grave closes and I am reunited with him." After the viewing and ceremonies at the state house had concluded, a long funeral procession carried the remains of Lincoln and his son to Oak Ridge Cemetery, on the northern edge of Springfield. There they were placed into a small receiving tomb dug into the hillside. In December the bodies were moved to another temporary vault higher up on the hill. On September 19, 1871, they were moved yet again. This time they were placed in a crypt at the great monument under construction. Tad Lincoln died that same year, on July 15, and was placed with his brother and father in the tomb.

In 1876 an attempt was made by three men to steal the body of Lincoln from its crypt and to hold it for ransom. The theft was foiled and the men involved jailed. Finally on September 26, 1901 measures were taken to prevent this from ever happening again. On that date the sarcophagus was dug up and cut open. Twenty three witnesses looked into the coffin and confirmed that it was indeed Lincoln. Then following the directions of Robert Lincoln, it was resealed and lowered into a pit 10 feet deep and covered with two tons of cement.

It was the last anyone would ever gaze upon the face of the man who led the country through the Civil War and who held our nation together. He was a man who forever changed and affected the lives of untold generations of Americans to come, Abraham Lincoln.

President Lincoln's Casket inside his Monument
at Oak Ridge Cemetery, Springfield, Ill.

COPYRIGHTED BY C. J. RESLER, TAYLORVILLE, ILL.

President Lincoln's casket, adorned with
flowers, is shown inside his monument at
Oak Ridge Cemetery in Springfield, Illinois.
c. 1912, C.J. Resler, Taylorville, OH [$6-8]

Seen in this postcard view is
the sarcophagus chamber inside the Lincoln Monument.
Abraham Lincoln's body
actually lies in a pit 10 feet
deep, covered in cement. In
the center of the room is a
cenotaph with the simple,
but fitting inscription, "Abraham Lincoln 1809-1865."
*Springfield News Agency,
Springfield, IL [$1-3]*

Chapter 5

Portraits & Photographs

In his autobiography, Lincoln wrote of his physical appearance, "I am, in height, six feet four inches, nearly; lean in flesh, weighing on average, one hundred and eighty pounds, dark complexion, with coarse black hair and grey eyes – no other marks or brands recollected." Fortunately for us today, the actual image of Abraham Lincoln was preserved and documented through the work of a number of professional photographers and portrait artists of his time.

According to Lloyd Ostendorff, noted expert on Lincoln photographs, there were 130 photographic portrait images made of Lincoln. The very first was taken in 1846 in Springfield, Illinois, when he was the newly elected Congressman from that state. The majority, 90, were taken after he was elected president in 1860 and began wearing a beard. In all he sat for some 36 different photographers during his lifetime, with Alexander Gardner being the most prolific. Many books state that it was Alexander Gardner who took the last photographic images of Lincoln in life, alleging that the pictures were taken on April 10, 1865. But documentation has shown that those images were in fact taken on February 5, 1865. It was a series of three photographs (one of which has been lost), taken on the balcony of the White House March 6, 1865 by Henry F. Warren, that were his final poses.

His likeness was also captured by portrait painters. Some portraits were made from life, as in the case of the artist Francis B. Carpenter, who spent six months living in the White House in 1864 painting the president. Most of the portraits we have today were drawn from photographs or from the artist's imagination. Whatever the source of the image, portraits of Lincoln have been very popular subjects on postcards.

Multiple photographic images of Abraham Lincoln from the years 1846-1865 show a transition in his appearance over the years.
c. 1910, B-H Publishing, Los Angeles,CA [$6-8]

Five portraits of Lincoln portray him at various stages of his life.
1908, W.M. Taggart, New York, NY [$6-8]

Images taken from numerous sources including postcards, currency, and postage stamps were used to create this montage.
c. 1960s, Publisher Unknown [$8-10]

A likeness of Abraham Lincoln apparently made from a photograph taken by Samuel M. Fasset on October, 4, 1859, in Chicago, Illinois.
c. 1959, W.M. Grandy, Warner,NH [$3-5]

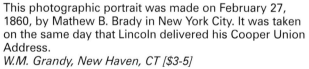

This photographic portrait was made on February 27, 1860, by Mathew B. Brady in New York City. It was taken on the same day that Lincoln delivered his Cooper Union Address.
W.M. Grandy, New Haven, CT [$3-5]

This photograph was taken by Alexander Hesler in Springfield, Illinois, on June 3, 1860, shortly after Lincoln's nomination as the Republican candidate for president.
Curteich, Chicago, IL [$2-4]

Lincoln said of this photograph, it "expresses me better than any I have ever seen; if it pleases the people I am satisfied." It was another photograph made by Alexander Hesler in Springfield on June 3, 1860.
c. 1960s, Sunburst Souvenirs [$2-3]

The work of Thomas Hicks (1823-1890), this oil painting is from the collection of the Chicago Historical Society. It was painted in June, 1860, in Springfield, Illinois.
c. 1960, Dexter Press, West Nyack, NY [$2-3]

A portrait of Lincoln made not long after his presidential nomination in 1860. Taken from an original crayon drawing from life, by artist Charles A. Barry (1830-1892). Originally intended for use on campaign posters it was however, rejected by the New York campaign chairman, who felt it not suitable for eastern voters.
c. 1910, Publisher unknown [$6-8]

Known as the "Smiling Lincoln," this was painted in Springfield just two months before the presidential election of 1860. The artist was Alban J. Conant (1821-1915).
Publisher unknown [$3-5]

This oil on canvas portrait, done from life, was made in Springfield, Illinois, in 1860. It is the work of the painter George P.A. Healey (1813-1894).
1959, Publisher unknown [$4-6]

A painted portrait of a beardless Lincoln done by Charles M. Shean (? –1925).
Publisher unknown [$3-5]

This is the first photograph of Lincoln with a full beard. It was taken in Springfield on January 13, 1861, by Christopher S. German.
c. 1908, Publisher unknown [$12-15]

ABRAHAM LINCOLN
One Hundredth Anniversary of his birth, February 12th, 1909

He said at Gettysburg:

"That we here highly resolve that the dead shall not have died in vain: that the nation shall, under God, have a new birth of Freedom, and that the Government of the people, by the people, and for the people, shall not perish from the earth."

On the day after arriving in Washington, D.C., as the new President-elect, Lincoln visited Mathew B. Brady's gallery to have a series of photographs taken. This is one of those images captured by photographer Alexander Gardner. The artist George H. Story posed Lincoln for the camera that day, February 24, 1861.
1909, Publisher unknown [$8-10]

An 1861 portrait of the Lincoln family in the White House painted by Francis B. Carpenter (1830-1900).
Publisher unknown [$4-6]

The Lincoln Family in 1861
painted by Francis B. Carpenter

The New-York Historical Society
Central Park W. at 77 St., N.Y.C.

This is a photograph taken by Mathew B. Brady at his Washington, D.C., gallery on April 6, 1861. The image was captured on an unusually large photographic plate measuring slightly over 18 by 20 inches.
c. 1914, Albertype Co., Brooklyn, NY [$6-8]

President Lincoln and Family in the White House.

The artist who painted this family portrait took some liberties with historical fact. Young Tad is seen with his mother's arm on his shoulder while Willie, who died on February 20, 1862, stands with a book near his father. Robert, the eldest son, is shown in military uniform even though he did not enter the army until 1865.
c. 1908, Majestic Publishing Co., Indianapolis, IN [$6-8]

The subject of this postcard is a painted portrait by George Henry Story (1835-1923). Story made several portraits of the president, who sat for him in the oval office over a three day period.
Metropolitan Engravers, Los Angeles, CA
[$5-7]

PRESIDENT LINCOLN

One of the better known sitting photographic portraits of the president, this likeness was captured by Alexander Gardner in Washington, D.C. on August 9, 1863.
© *1907, Buckingham & Harley, Washington, D.C.*
[$12-14]

Abraham Lincoln

A painted portrait based on an Alexander Gardner's photograph taken on November 8, 1863.
1955, Curteich, Chicago, IL [$2-4]

Considered one of the best images of Lincoln, this photograph was taken by Alexander Gardner on November 8, 1863, in Washington, D.C. It was only 11 days before the president delivered his famous Gettysburg Address.
Leib Image Archives, York, PA [$1-3]

This is an artist's drawing of Tad Lincoln on one of his two ponies. It is based on a photograph made by H.F. Warren on November 16, 1863. The artist added the president to the picture. Sadly both of Tad's ponies were later killed in a White House stable fire on February 10, 1864.
© 1906, Viola H. Gibon(?) [$6-8]

A painted portrait by an unknown artist.
1934, Curteich, Chicago, IL [$3-5]

LINCOLN, THE PRESIDENT

4A-H1186

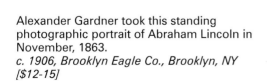

Artist Allen C. Redwood (1844-1922) created this depiction of Lincoln on horseback. It probably represents the president on one of his many rides to the Soldier's Home just outside Washington.
W.M. Grandy, New Haven, CT [$2-4]

Alexander Gardner took this standing photographic portrait of Abraham Lincoln in November, 1863.
c. 1906, Brooklyn Eagle Co., Brooklyn, NY [$12-15]

8o88.   ABRAHAM LINCOLN.

In this painting, an artist has captured the likeness of Lincoln standing with the Capitol dome in the background.
c. 1907, Publisher unknown [$4-6]

A painting based on a famous photographic portrait taken by Mathew B. Brady at his studio in Washington on February 9, 1864. This is the image seen today on our $5 bill.
c. 1908, Robbins Bros., Boston, MA [$4-6]

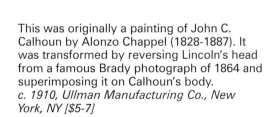

A portrait adapted from the Brady photograph taken on February 9, 1864.
c. 1907, Publisher unknown [$4-6]

This was originally a painting of John C. Calhoun by Alonzo Chappel (1828-1887). It was transformed by reversing Lincoln's head from a famous Brady photograph of 1864 and superimposing it on Calhoun's body.
c. 1910, Ullman Manufacturing Co., New York, NY [$5-7]

Portrait made from life by the artist
Francis B. Carpenter in 1864.
c. 1959, W.M. Grandy, Warner, NH
[$3-5]

1809-1865

A seated portrait by an
unknown artist.
*1906, Detroit Publishing
Co., Detroit, MI [$6-8]*

Based on photographs of the president,
the artist William E. Marshall (1837-1906)
painted this portrait in 1864.
Arthur Jaffe Heliochrome Co., New York, NY
[$4-6]

This is one of several portraits and studies
of Abraham Lincoln painted by Douglas Volk
(1856-1935). The artist's father, Leonard Volk,
is famous for his life mask of Lincoln made in
1860.
c. 1930s, Publisher unknown [$6-8]

Farragut   Sherman   Hancock   Thomas   Grant   Meade   Sheridan
                                            Lincoln   Hooker

Lincoln and his Generals: The famous Civil War group.

A painting portraying Lincoln with some of his more famous generals. Among those included with the president are Generals Grant, Meade, Sheridan, and Sherman.
c. 1910, Publisher unknown [$6-8]

The artist Francis H. Schell (1834-1909) painted this Lincoln family portrait. It is based on a photograph of Lincoln and his son Tad, taken by Anthony Berger at Mathew Brady's studio on February 9, 1864. The artist added Robert and Mary Lincoln to the original picture. Engravings of this painting became very popular after the death of the president.
c.1908, W.M. Taggart, New York, NY [$10-12]

The Last Photograph the President Sat for.   34

On February 5, 1865 Alexander Gardner took a number of photographs of the president. In this image, Lincoln is posed with his son Tad in front of an ornamental background.
c. 1910, Publisher unknown [$8-10]

In this photograph Lincoln sits with spectacles and a pencil in his hands. Alexander Gardner took this picture along with a number of others during the president's last formal sitting on February 5, 1865.
c. 1960, Curteich, Chicago, IL [$6-8]

1809—LINCOLN CENTENARY—1909

SPRINGFIELD HOME.

Every man is said to have his peculiar ambition. Whether that be true or not, I can say, for one, that I have no other so great as that of being truly esteemed of my fellow-men, by rendering myself worthy of their esteem. —*From a speech, 1832.*

LINCOLN DURING HIS PRESIDENCY.
From a photograph by Brady.

TOMB.

Copyright, 1908, BY THE CENTURY CO.

"ABRAHAM LINCOLN" BY PETER BAUMGRAS, 1865
McLELLAN LINCOLN COLLECTION
BROWN UNIVERSITY LIBRARY

Incorrectly identified on this postcard as a photograph taken by Mathew Brady, this portrait was actually made by Lewis Emory Walker in February of 1865. It shows Lincoln with his hair uncharacteristically standing almost straight up. The image was originally published as a stereograph.
© 1908, The Century Co. [$8-10]

Shortly before his assassination in April of 1865, the president sat for this portrait by Peter Baumgras (1827-1904)..
The painting is now part of the Lincoln collection at Brown University.
Artvue Post Card Co., New York, NY [$4-6]

ABRAHAM LINCOLN — PAINTING BY G. P. A. HEALY
CHICAGO HISTORICAL SOCIETY

The last painted life portrait of Lincoln was this oil painting by Matthew Wilson (1814-1892). It was dated April 1865, the month Lincoln was assassinated.
c. 1960s, Publisher unknown, [$2-4]

The artist G.P.A. Healey (1813-1894) used photographs of Lincoln as the basis for his painting titled *The Meeting on the River Queen*, of which this is a part. Lincoln met with Generals Grant and Sherman, and Admiral Porter, on board the steamboat *River Queen* on March 27, 1865.
Artvue Post Card Co., New York,NY [$4-6]

This portrait engraving of Abraham Lincoln is believed to be the work of William E. Marshall (1837-1906). It was one of the most widely distributed images of Lincoln following his death in 1865.
c. 1910, J. Koehler, New York, NY [$6-8]

COPYRIGHT, J. KOEHLER, N. Y.
ABRAHAM LINCOLN

Chapter Six

His Lasting Words

When it came to using the written or spoken word, Abraham Lincoln was a master. It was an ability he learned and developed over his years in pursuing a career in law and politics. Even as a young man he had a talent for expertly relating humorous stories and anecdotes to help illustrate his message. He would become equally adept at communicating thoughtful, emotional, and powerful sentiments through the use of his words. This was true whether it was in his correspondence, speeches, or conversations. Fortunately for us today, many of his words have been preserved in written form. Some of his writings and speeches, especially those related to important issues of his day, are considered to be among the greatest in our nation's history.

There is an abundance of quotations attributed to Lincoln. However there are also some for which he has been falsely given credit. The following postcards give us a sampling of some of his more notable and famous words, words that in many instances are as meaningful today as when spoken or written in the 19th Century by the great man himself.

In speaking of his ambition, Lincoln said that he wished to be "truly esteemed of my fellow men, by rendering myself worthy of their esteem." He spoke these words in an address given on March 9, 1832, while seeking election to the Illinois General Assembly. It was an election that he lost.
1908, M.T. Sheahan, Boston, MA [$4-6]

Said to be a religious man by nature, Lincoln was a reader of the Bible and often quoted from it. However, he never joined an organized church. This is a quotation regarding his views on what an ideal church should be.
1908, M.T. Sheahan, Boston, MA [$4-6]

The portraits above that of Lincoln are of his father Thomas and his mother Nancy Hanks Lincoln. In a conversation with his law partner William Herndon, Lincoln is quoted as saying "all that I am, or all that I hope to be I owe to my angel mother."
© *1908, M.T. Sheahan, Boston, MA [$5-7]*

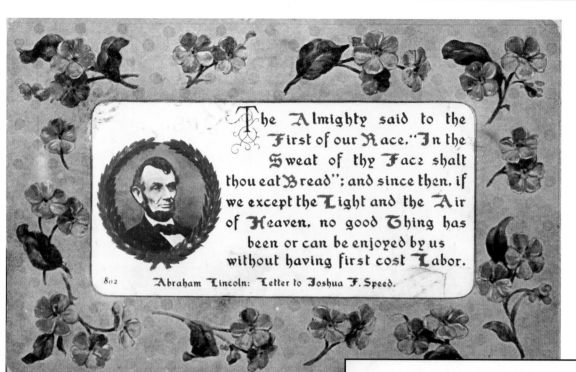

In a letter to his long-time friend Joshua Speed written on December 1, 1847(?), Lincoln wrote that "no good thing has been or can be enjoyed by us without having first cost labor."
1908, Franz Huld Co., New York, NY [$4-6]

"The leading rule for the man of every calling is diligence." This quote is from "Notes for a Law Lecture." According to his secretaries Nicolay and Hay, it was dated July 1, 1850.
© *1908, M.T. Sheahan, Boston, MA [$5-7]*

A snowstorm on February 27, 1860 in New York City did not keep some 1,500 people from hearing Abraham Lincoln's speech at the Cooper Union Hall. This address, heard by some of the most influential men in the city, helped propel him to national attention. The date of that speech is incorrectly printed on this postcard.
c. 1908, Anglo American Co., New York, NY [$20-25]

The famous words "Let us have faith that right makes might" come from the Cooper Union Address made on February 27, 1860. In his speech, Lincoln pointed out the Republican Party's need to stand by their opposition to the expansion of slavery.
c. 1910, Anglo American Co., [$20-25]

Before departing Springfield for Washington, D.C., to be inaugurated as president, Lincoln gave a short address to the crowd from the rear platform of his railroad car. These words come from that speech given on February 11, 1861.
© 1908, M.T. Sheahan, Boston, MA [$4-6]

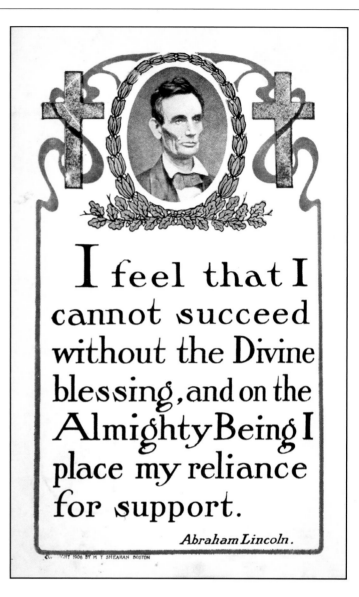

"I am not ashamed to confess that 25 years ago I was a hired laborer." These words were part of a speech in which Lincoln expressed his views on the rights of laboring men. It was given in New Haven, Connecticut, on March 6, 1860.
1908, M.T. Sheahan, Boston, MA [$5-7]

In his first Inaugural Address on March 4, 1861, Lincoln stated that his oath was a "solemn one to preserve and defend" the government. He knew that the greatest challenge facing him was going to be holding the nation together. *c. 1910, Anglo American Co., New York, NY {$20-25]*

On August 22, 1862 Lincoln wrote a letter to the noted newspaper editor and founder of the New York *Tribune*, Horace Greeley. This letter was in response to Greeley's writing in his newspaper that Lincoln was not doing enough "to fight slavery with liberty." The president finished his letter by declaring his personal "oft expressed wish that all men everywhere should be free." At the time, Lincoln had a draft of the Emancipation Proclamation in his desk waiting an opportune time to make it public. *c. 1910, Anglo American Co., New York, NY {$20-25]*

By "giving freedom to the slaves we insure freedom to the free…"This was part of Abraham Lincoln's annual message to Congress, which he delivered on December 1, 1862. *c. 1910, Anglo American Co., New York, NY [$20-25]*

Chapter 6: His Lasting Words

The Emancipation Proclamation is considered to be one of the most important documents of Lincoln's presidency. It went into effect on January 1, 1863.
c. 1920, Publisher Unknown {$6-8]

LINCOLN'S ADDRESS
Delivered at Gettysburg, Nov. 19, 1863

Fourscore and seven years ago our fathers brought forth on this continent a new nation, conceived in liberty, and dedicated to the proposition that all men are created equal. Now we are engaged in a great civil war, testing whether that nation, or any nation so conceived and so dedicated can long endure.— We are met on a great battlefield of that war. We have come to dedicate a portion of that field, as a final resting place for those who here gave their lives that that nation might live. It is altogether fitting and proper that we should do this. But in a larger sense we cannot dedicate, we cannot consecrate, we cannot hallow this ground. The brave men, living and dead, who struggled here, have consecrated it far above our poor power to add or detract. The world will little note, nor long remember, what we say here; but it can never forget what they did here. It is for us the living, rather, to be dedicated here to the unfinished work which they who fought here have thus far so nobly advanced. It is rather for us to be dedicated to the great task remaining before us — that from these honored dead we take increased devotion to that cause for which they gave the last full measure of devotion — that we here highly resolve that these dead shall not have died in vain — that this nation, under God, shall have a new birth of freedom — and that government of the people, by the people, and for the people shall not perish from the earth.

WILLS HOUSE, where Address was written

SOLDIERS' NATIONAL CEMETERY
GETTYSBURG, where address was delivered

Abraham Lincoln is known to have penned five copies of the Gettysburg Address. The first of these is known as the Washington copy, while the second, the Wills copy, was completed in Gettysburg. In 1864, Lincoln wrote out three other drafts. It is the fifth and only copy signed by him that has become the standard version. Known as the Bliss copy, it now hangs in the Lincoln Room of the White House.
c. 1908, Publisher unknown [$5-7]

LINCOLN'S ADDRESS
Delivered at Gettysburg, Pa.
Nov. 19, 1863

"Fourscore and seven years ago our fathers brought forth on this continent a new nation, conceived in liberty, and dedicated to the proposition that all men are created equal. ** Now we are engaged in a great civil war, testing whether that nation, or any nation so conceived and so dedicated, can long endure. ** We are met on a great battle-field of that war. * We have come to dedicate a portion of that field as a final resting place for those who here gave their lives that that nation might live. **** It is altogether fitting and proper that we should do this. But in a larger sense we cannot dedicate, we cannot consecrate, we cannot hallow this ground. The brave men, living and dead, who struggled here, have consecrated it far above our poor power to add or detract. ** The world will little note, nor long remember, what we say here, but it can never forget what they did here. It is for us, the living, rather to be dedicated here to the unfinished work which they who fought here have thus far so nobly advanced. ** It is rather for us to be here dedicated to the great task remaining before us, that from these honored dead we take increased devotion to that cause for which they gave the last full measure of devotion; that we here highly resolve that these dead shall not have died in vain; that this nation, under God, shall have a new birth of freedom, and that the government of the people, by the people, and for the people shall not perish from the earth."

Freedom

These are the immortal words to the Gettysburg Address. It was on November 19, 1863, at the dedication ceremonies for the National Military Cemetery in Gettysburg that Lincoln delivered what is perhaps his most famous speech.
c. 1942, Tichnor Bros., Inc., Boston, MA [$2-4]

"The government of the people, by the
people, and for the people, shall not
perish from the earth."

A. Lincoln

79 Pub by S. W. Lewis, Merchantville, N. J.

This postcard quotes one of the more familiar lines from the Gettysburg Address. "The
government of the people, by the people,
and for the people, shall not perish from the
earth."
*c. 1904, S.W. Lewis, Merchantville, NJ [$4-
6]*

Four-
score and seven
years ago our fathers
brought forth on this continent a
new nation, con-   ceived in liberty
and dedicated   to the proposition that   all men are created
equal.   Now we are engaged in
a   great civil war, testing
                          whether that nation or any
                          nation so conceived and so
                          dedicated, can long endure.
tle   We are met on a great bat-
come to   field of that war. We have
as a fi-   dedicate a portion of that field
who   nal resting-place of those
                          here gave their lives that that
                          nation might live. It is alto-
                      gether fit ting and proper
                      that we should do this. But
                  in a larg- er   sense we,
                  cannot dedi-   cate ----- we
                  cannot conse-   crate ----- we
                  can-   not hallow -----
                          this ground. The brave
                          men, living and dead
who   strug gle d here, have
con-   secrated it, far above
our poor power   to add or de- tract. The
world will little   note, nor long   re- member, what we say here, but   it
can never forget what they   did
here. It is for us the liv-   ing, rather to be   dedicated here to
to the   unfinished work which
they who   fought here have thus far
so nobly advanced. It is rather for us to be here
dedicated   to the great task remaining before us----
that from these honored dead we take increased devotion to that cause for which they gave the last full measure of devotion----that we here highly resolve that these dead
shall   not have died in vain----that this nation, under God,
shall   have a new birth of freedom----and that government   of the people, by the people, and for the people
shall   not perish from the earth. This address was de-
liv- ered at the dedication of Gettysburg   Cemetery, Gettysburg,   Pennsylvania, No-   vem-
ber 19, 1863.   This speech
is admired by
all.

Commemorating the Gettysburg Address,
November 19, 1863.

An image of Abraham Lincoln formed by the
words to his Gettysburg Address.
Lincoln Exhibits, Winter Park, FL [$2-3]

The quotation given on this card is, perhaps, a paraphrasing of a remark Lincoln made to his secretary John Hay on December 24, 1863. He is reported to have actually said, "Common looking people are the best in the world, that is the reason the Lord made so many of them."
c. 1910, Publisher unknown [$6-8]

"When a man is sincerely penitent…he can be safely pardoned." This was taken from remarks made to a White House visitor in regards to the Amnesty Proclamation of April 30, 1864.
1908, Franz Huld Co., New York, NY [$4-6]

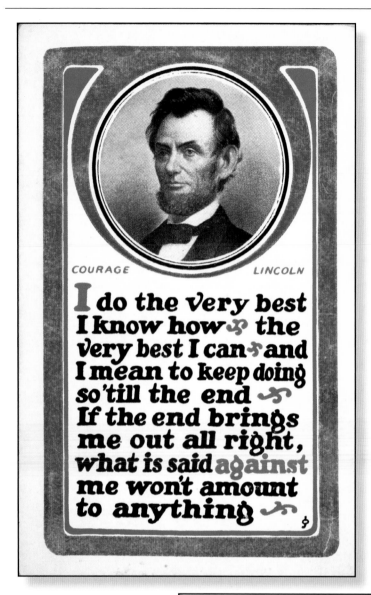

"I do the very best I know how…" These words have been attributed to Abraham Lincoln by the painter Francis Carpenter who spent time living in the White House. Carpenter relates this quote in his book *Six Months at the White House*, which was published in 1867.
1908, M.T. Sheahan, Boston, MA [$4-6]

On November 10, 1864, in response to a serenade given to him at the White House, Lincoln gave a short address. In discussing the importance of holding a presidential election during a time of civil war, he commented that "living brave and patriotic men are better than gold."
c. 1910, Metropolitan Post Card Co., Everett, MA [$3-5]

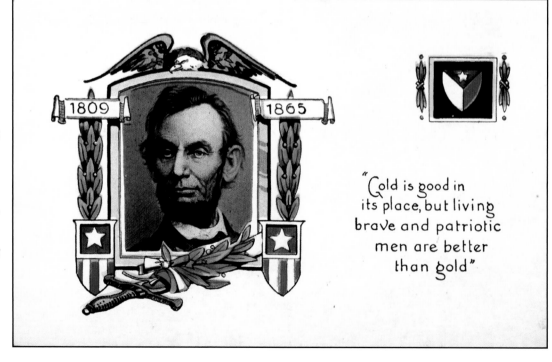

These words were spoken to his long time friend Joshua Speed, who was visiting the White House in February of 1865. Lincoln stated that "I want it said of me...that I always plucked a thistle and planted a flower."
c. 1904, United Order of the Golden Cross [$4-6]

One of Lincoln's most famous speeches was his Second Inaugural Address, given on March 4, 1865. With victory in the war within sight, he called upon his fellow countrymen to help "bind up the nation's wounds"
c. 1909, Womens Trust Union League, New York, NY [$5-7]

"With malice toward none, with charity for all…" A memorable line from the Second Inaugural Address.
© 1906, The Rotograph Co., New York, NY [$8-10]

You cannot bring about prosperity by discouraging thrift.

You cannot strengthen the weak by weakening the strong.

You cannot help the wage earner by pulling down the wage payer.

You cannot further the brotherhood of man by encouraging class hatred.

You cannot help the poor by destroying the rich.

You cannot keep out of trouble by spending more than you earn.

You cannot build character and courage by taking away man's initiative and independence.

You cannot help men permanently by doing for them what they could and should do for themselves.

Abraham Lincoln

These eight statements have often been associated with Abraham Lincoln. They are in fact taken from a list of 10 statements written by Rev. William J.H. Boetcker in 1916. It is an excellent example of quotes falsely attributed to Lincoln.
Columbia View Cards, Ocean Park, WA [$2-3]

"You may fool all of the people some of the time..." This is another well known quotation often attributed to Abraham Lincoln.
© 1908, The Century Co., New York, NY [$8-10]

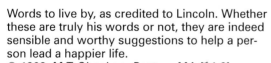

Words to live by, as credited to Lincoln. Whether these are truly his words or not, they are indeed sensible and worthy suggestions to help a person lead a happier life.
© 1908, M.T. Sheahan, Boston, MA [$4-6]

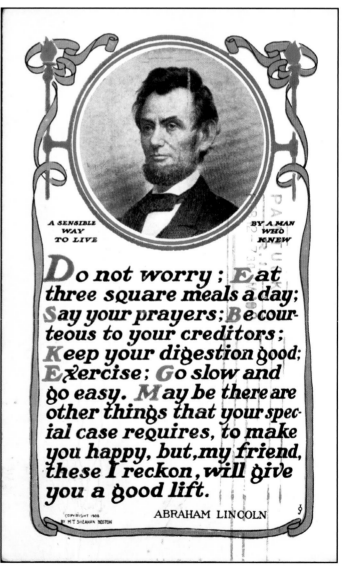

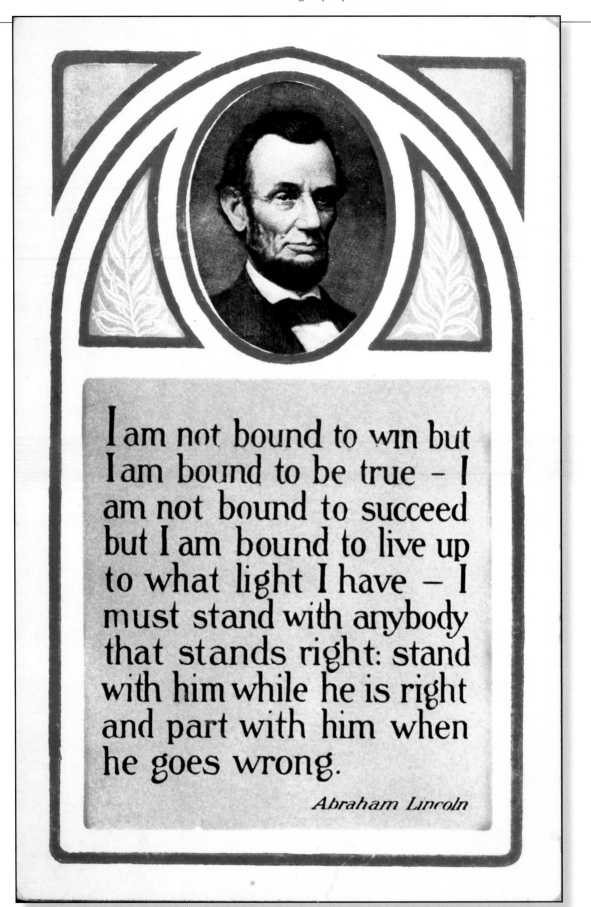

"I am not bound to win but I am bound to be true ..." A quotation which has been attributed
to Abraham Lincoln and said to express his principles regarding standing up for what is right.
c. 1908, M.T. Sheahan, Boston, MA [$4-6]

Chapter 7

Monuments & Memorials

After the body of the martyred president was laid to rest and the shock and grief over his death had passed, his memory did not fade. In fact the name of Abraham Lincoln and his image, have become pervasive in our history and culture. More books have been written about this man than any other American. Some 34 American cities bear his name, as do countless schools, colleges, streets, highways, bridges, buildings, and businesses. We encounter his image on our currency and postage stamps. And in some states his birthday is celebrated as a legal holiday.

Since his death, his birthplace, family home sites, and various buildings associated with his life have been preserved as National Historic Sites. It was not long after his passing that monuments and memorials began to appear throughout the nation. In town squares, city parks, on college campuses, and public lands, hundreds of sculptures and statues of all types were erected. Made of granite, marble, bronze, or other materials, they all pay homage to this man, his works, or the principles he stood for. From small plaques to the massive and impressive National Lincoln Memorial, all of these remembrances cause us to pause and contemplate the impact Abraham Lincoln has had on our nation and society. He was a man who rose from humble beginnings to become one of the greatest names in American history.

5446. LINCOLN MONUMENT, LINCOLN PARK, CHICAGO.

ILLINOIS – Chicago. One of the most famous statues honoring Lincoln is that located in Chicago's Lincoln Park. Sculpted by Augustus Saint-Gaudens, it was unveiled to the public on October 22, 1887.
© 1907, E. Phillips [$3-5]

ILLINOIS – Dixon. Dedicated on August 23, 1930, this bronze statue titled *Lincoln the Soldier*, is the work of sculptor Leonard Crunelle. Lincoln is portrayed as he may have looked when he served as a Captain of Volunteers during the Black Hawk War. *Color-View Inc., Rockford, IL [$1-3]*

ILLINOIS – Freeport. A monument marks the location where Abraham Lincoln and Stephen A. Douglas debated on August 27, 1858. President Theodore Roosevelt dedicated this memorial in 1903.
c. 1909, W.C. Ruch, Freeport, IL [$6-8]

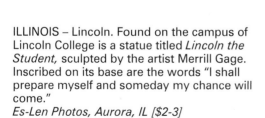

Lincoln Memorial, Freeport, Ill.

ILLINOIS – Freeport. This statue titled *Lincoln the Debater* is the work of Leonard Crunello. It memorializes Lincoln's second debate with Stephen A. Douglas, which was held in this town.
c. 1946, Curteich, Chicago, IL [$2-4]

ILLINOIS – Lincoln. Found on the campus of Lincoln College is a statue titled *Lincoln the Student,* sculpted by the artist Merrill Gage. Inscribed on its base are the words "I shall prepare myself and someday my chance will come."
Es-Len Photos, Aurora, IL [$2-3]

ILLINOIS – Petersburg. Standing at the entrance to New Salem State Park is this nine foot tall bronze likeness of a young Abraham Lincoln. Sculpted by Avard Fairbanks, it depicts Lincoln discarding his ax and taking up his law books. This statue was presented to the people of Illinois in 1954.
Springfield News Agency, Springfield, IL [$2-3]

ILLINOIS – Quincy. A memorial plaque fixed to marble marks the site of the sixth Lincoln and Douglas debate, which was held on October 13, 1858. It is found in what is now the city's Washington Park.
c. 1930, E.C. Kropp Co., Milwaukee, WI [$2-4]

ILLINOIS – Springfield. This magnificent memorial in Oak Ridge Cemetery stands above the tomb of Abraham Lincoln. The obelisk, which stands 117 feet tall, is surrounded by four large bronze groupings at its base. Each grouping represents a different branch of the military. Standing there also is a statue of Lincoln.
c. 1910, Publisher unknown [$3-5]

BRONZE FIGURES ON LINCOLN'S MONUMENT IN OAKRIDGE CEMETERY, SPRINGFIELD, ILL.

ILLINOIS – Springfield. One of the sculpted bronze groupings on the monument is this one titled *Cavalry Group.* It represents a battle scene in which a wounded trumpeter has been thrown from his horse and is being aided by a comrade. Like the others on the memorial it is the work of the artist Larkin G. Mead, Jr.
c. 1910, Hammon Publishing Co., Chicago, IL [$4-6]

ILLINOIS – Springfield. The chamber inside the monument in Oak Ridge Cemetery contains a cenotaph surrounded by nine state flags representing all of the states in which the Lincoln family lived since arriving in this country. Lincoln's body lies buried under the floor near the north wall.
c. 1930, H.N. Shonkwiler, Springfield, IL [$2-4]

ILLINOIS – Springfield. Shown inside the tomb is a small museum with artifacts from his life and exhibits honoring his deeds. This museum was removed in the early 1930s and the space is now utilized as the entrance rotunda.
c. 1930, H.N. Shonkwiler, Springfield, IL [$3-5]

ILLINOIS – Springfield. In front of the Illinois State Capitol stands a sculpture of Lincoln by Andrew O'Connor. Dedicated on October 5, 1918, it commemorated the centennial of the state's first General Assembly.
1953, Curteich, Chicago, IL [$1-3]

INDIANA – Fort Wayne. Titled *The Hoosier Youth*, this bronze statue by Paul H. Manship, stands at the entrance to the Lincoln National Life Insurance home office. It represents Lincoln as he may have looked when he lived in Indiana. Dedication ceremonies were held on September 16, 1932.
c. 1960s, Marquart Camera Shop, Fort Wayne, IN [$2-4]

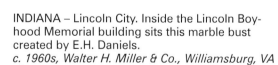

INDIANA – Lincoln City. The Lincoln Boyhood National Memorial is a tribute to Abraham Lincoln and his mother Nancy Hanks Lincoln. Materials for the building's construction all came from Indiana. There are five large sculptured panels, all the work of sculptor E.H. Daniels, depicting scenes from Lincoln's life.
c. 1960s, Walter H. Miller & Co., Williamsburg, VA
[$1-3]

INDIANA – Lincoln City. Inside the Lincoln Boyhood Memorial building sits this marble bust created by E.H. Daniels.
c. 1960s, Walter H. Miller & Co., Williamsburg, VA
[$1-3]

INDIANA – Lincoln City. In 1917 this simple monument was placed at the site where the Lincoln cabin once stood. The family lived there from 1816-1830.
c. 1928, C. Bever [$4-6]

INDIANA – Lincoln City. During the 1930s, 300 hearthstones were excavated from the site of the old Lincoln cabin. These stones were used to construct a wall around the spot and a new bronze marker was put in place.
1952, Curteich, Chicago, IL [$3-5]

Home of Abraham Lincoln, Years 1816 to 1830

Lincoln Homestead, Lincoln City, Spencer County, Indiana

INDIANA – Vincennes. On the Illinois side of the Lincoln Memorial Bridge is a monument marking the spot where the Lincoln family first entered Illinois from Indiana in 1830.
1939, Curteich, Chicago, IL [$3-5]

Memorial Marking Spot where Lincoln Family entered Illinois from Indiana 1830

"GOD BLESS MY MOTHER. ALL THAT I AM OR EVER HOPE TO BE, I OWE TO MY ANGEL MOTHER." A. LINCOLN

Located Illinois Side of Lincoln Memorial Bridge, Vincennes, Ind.

*Abraham Lincoln Memorial, Lincoln Park
Entrance to Rohrer Park Residence District
at Oakland Drive, Council Bluffs, Iowa.*

IOWA – Council Bluffs. The granite pylon erected in July of 1911 commemorates Lincoln's visit to this site in 1859. From here Lincoln viewed and selected the location for the Eastern Terminus of the Transcontinental Railroad. In the 1990s the monument was restored.
Eric Nelson News Co., Omaha, NE [$4-6]

IOWA – Des Moines. Lincoln and his son Tad, sculpted larger than life size, are the work of Fred and Mabel Torrey. Dedicated in 1961 it is found on the Iowa State Capitol grounds.
c. 1960s, Hurley's Supply Co., Des Moines, IA [$2-4]

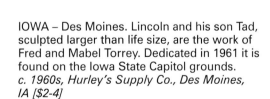

IOWA – Sioux City. A likeness of Lincoln stands at the entrance to Grandview Park. Unveiled April 5, 1924, this bronze work of art was created by W. Granville Hastings. An identical statue can be found in Cincinnati, Ohio.
General Tobacco Co., Sioux City, IA [$2-4]

KANSAS –Topeka. Located on the grounds of the State House in Topeka, this memorial titled *The Man of Sorrow*, is the work of artist Merrill Gage.
c. 1940, Theo. Zercher, Topeka, KS [$2-4]

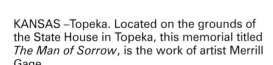

LINCOLN MEMORIAL HALL ON LINCOLN FARM, NEAR HODGENVILLE, KY.

67247

KENTUCKY – Hodgenville. On the site of the Sinking Spring Farm where Lincoln was born, stands this Greek temple-like memorial. Designed by architect John Russell Pope, it was constructed between 1909-1911. Its 56 steps leading to the entrance symbolize each year in Lincoln's life. Inside is a reconstruction of the cabin in which he was born.
Curteich, Chicago, IL [$2-4]

LINCOLN

KENTUCKY – Hodgenville. A seated Lincoln sculpted by Adolph A. Weinman and cast in bronze, was dedicated Memorial Day, May 31, 1909. It is located in the town square of Hodgenville. There is a copy of this statue on the campus of the University of Wisconsin.
c. 1956, Curteich, Chicago, IL [$1-3]

Lincoln Monument, Park Square, Boston, Mass.

MASSACHUSETTS – Boston. A duplicate of the *Emancipation Statue* found in Washington D.C., this bronze sculpture is the work of Thomas Ball. It was dedicated on December 6, 1879.
c. 1918, Reichner Bros., Boston, MA [$4-6]

MASSACHUSETTS – Hingham. Samuel Lincoln, the first of Abraham Lincoln's ancestors to arrive in this country, settled here in Hingham, Massachusetts in 1637. This monument to our 16th President was dedicated in September of 1939. It is located at the corner of North and Lincoln Streets.
Bromley & Co., Boston, MA [$2-4]

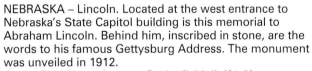

MASSACHUSETTS – Lowell. Proceeds from the sale of this postcard, published in 1908, went towards the expenses of erecting this memorial. The monument stands several hundred feet from the Lincoln Elementary School on Chelmsford Street.
© 1908, Abraham Lincoln Memorial Committee, Lowell, MA [$5-7]

NEBRASKA – Lincoln. Located at the west entrance to Nebraska's State Capitol building is this memorial to Abraham Lincoln. Behind him, inscribed in stone, are the words to his famous Gettysburg Address. The monument was unveiled in 1912.
Springfield News Agency, Springfield, IL [$1-3]

NEBRASKA – Lincoln. This is the original plaster cast of the bronze statue that was installed at the state capitol. Titled *Abraham Lincoln at Gettysburg, 1864*, it is the work of the famous sculptor Daniel Chester French.
Art Institute of Chicago, Chicago, IL [$4-6]

NEW JERSEY – Newark. Sculpted by Gutzon Borglum (the carver of Mt. Rushmore), this informal pose of Lincoln was dedicated by President Theodore Roosevelt in 1911. Its located at the Essex County Courthouse in Newark.
c. 1918, Union News Co., Washington, D.C. [$4-6]

NEW YORK – Brooklyn. This statue of a standing Lincoln is located in Prospect Park.
c. 1905, The Rotograph Co., New York, NY [$6-8]

NEW YORK – New York City. Unveiled on September 16, 1870, this larger than life statue is the work of Henry Kirke Brown. Here it is seen at the southwest corner of Union Square. In 1930 it was moved to the north end of the square and the ornate fence was removed.
© 1905, The Rotograph Co., New York, NY [$6-8]

OHIO – Alliance. The stone used to build this memorial was taken from the Lincoln farm in Kentucky. A bronze plaque commemorates the fact that Lincoln stopped here during his trip to Washington to be inaugurated. He spoke briefly to people who gathered at this railroad station on February 15, 1861.
Kelley Studios, Hagerstown, MD [$1-3]

LINCOLN STATUE, AVONDALE, CINCINNATI, OHIO.

OHIO – Cincinnati. Unveiled on December 23, 1902, this 19 foot tall statue of Lincoln with Lady Liberty below him, is the work of William Granville Hastings. Belonging to the Cincinnati Public School System, it is located on the grounds of the South Avondale Elementary School.
c. 1915, The Feicke-Desch Co., Cincinnati, OH [$3-5]

OHIO – Columbus. A marble bust of Lincoln placed above a relief commemorating the capture of Vicksburg, stands in the Ohio State Capitol rotunda.
1907, David S. Ireland [$8-10]

PENNSYLVANIA – Gettysburg. Erected in 1912, this monument is dedicated to Lincoln's most famous speech. Its semicircular form has two bronze panels. The panels are inscribed with the words of David Wills's invitation to speak at the dedication ceremonies for the National Military Cemetery and also the words to Lincoln's Gettysburg Address. It is located just inside the west entrance to the National Cemetery.
c. 1916, The Inter-State News Co. [$3-5]

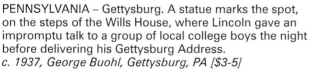

ABRAHAM LINCOLN ADDRESSED COLLEGE BOYS FROM THE STEPS OF THE WILLS HOUSE ON THE EVENING OF NOVEMBER 18, 1863

PENNSYLVANIA – Gettysburg. A statue marks the spot, on the steps of the Wills House, where Lincoln gave an impromptu talk to a group of local college boys the night before delivering his Gettysburg Address.
c. 1937, George Buohl, Gettysburg, PA [$3-5]

PENNSYLVANIA – Gettysburg. On a sidewalk in the town square stands this statue by J. Seward Johnson, Jr. Titled *Return Visit*, it shows Lincoln directing a modern tourist to the room in the Wills House where he completed writing his Gettysburg Address.
c. 1992, The Lane Studio, Gettysburg, PA [$2-4]

№ 16. Lincoln's Statue, Philadelphia, Pa.

PENNSYLVANIA – Philadelphia. This highly detailed bronze likeness of the martyred president is a well known landmark in Philadelphia's Fairmount Park. The work of Randolph Rogers, it shows a seated Lincoln holding a copy of the Emancipation Proclamation. An estimated 50,000 people witnessed its unveiling in 1871.
c. 1905, American Historical Art Co., New York, NY [$6-8]

49—Mt. Rushmore Memorial, Black Hills, S. D.

SOUTH DAKOTA – Black Hills. Carved into the side of Mt. Rushmore are the faces of four of our nation's great presidents. Begun in 1927 by the sculptor Gutzon Borglum, it took 400 workers 14 years to complete, due to delays caused by weather and lack of funding. The final cost of the project was $900,000.
1946, Curteich, Chicago, IL [$2-4]

48—Face of Abraham Lincoln, Mt. Rushmore National Memorial

Black Hills, So. Dak.

SOUTH DAKOTA – Black Hills. The third face to be completed, Lincoln's stone portraiture was dedicated September 17, 1937. Sixty feet in height from chin to top of his head; it is the largest image of our 16th president.
1948, Curteich, Chicago, IL [$2-4]

VERMONT – Bennington. Called the *Spirit of America*, this artwork was displayed at the World's Fair in 1939 before being placed in the courtyard of the Bennington Museum.
c. 1960s, Forward's Color Productions, Manchester, VT [$3-5]

WASHINGTON – Spokane. Dedicated on November 11, 1930, the statue situated at Main and Monroe Streets is the work of sculptor Alonzo Victor Lewis.
1948, Keenan News Agency, Spokane, WA [$2-4]

WISCONSIN – Kenoha. A bronze seated Lincoln with legs crossed is the work of Charles H. Niehous. It is a copy of a similar work found in Buffalo, New York. The statue was unveiled in 1909 and is found in the city's Library Park.
1909, J.M. Pull [$6-8]

WISCONSIN – Racine. Revealed to the public on February 12, 1924, this sculpture by Van den Bergen, stands at 2015 Prospect Street in Racine. A copy of this statue can be found in Clinton, Iowa.
E.A. Bishop Publishing, Racine, WI [$3-5]

2002—Lincoln-Todd Monument Racine, Wisconsin

MARY TODD   ABRAHAM

LINCOLN

4B-H1198

WISCONSIN – Racine. Located in the city's East Park, this statue depicting a seated Abraham Lincoln with his wife Mary Todd standing beside him, was dedicated on July 4, 1943. When local resident, Miss Lena Rosewall died in 1935, she left $20,000 in her will to pay for the creation of this sculpture. It is the work of Chicago artist Frederick C. Hibbard. *1944, Curteich, Chicago, IL [$2-4]*

WYOMING – Cheyenne. This monument is located near the top of Sherman Hill along Interstate 80, between Cheyenne and Laramie. It was placed here in 1969.
c. 1975, R&T Card Service, Cheyenne, WY [$2-3]

WASHINGTON, D.C. The first public monument to be dedicated to Abraham Lincoln was unveiled on the third anniversary of his assassination, April 14, 1868. The work of the Irish sculptor Lot Flannery, this memorial stood in front of the old City Hall on D Street until 1919. After restoration, it was reinstalled without its tall column in 1922.
c. 1909, C.E. Wheelock & Co., Peoria, IL [$5-7]

Lincoln Monument and City Hall, Washington, D. C.

Lincoln Statue. Washington, D. C.

No. 780   Published by The Washington News Company, Washington, D. C.-Leipzig-Berlin

WASHINGTON, D.C. Known as the Freedom's Memorial, this bronze monument is found in Lincoln Park. Sculpted by Thomas Ball, the funds for the statue came from freed slaves who donated the money to honor the "Great Emancipator." It was dedicated in 1876.
c. 1904, Washington News Co., Washington, D.C. [$6-8]

WASHINGTON, D.C. Located in the rotunda of the United States Capitol building, this marble statue was unveiled on January 25, 1871. It is the work of Vinnie Ream, who while a teenager, was able to sketch the president during the last five months of his life.
c. 1950s, Publisher unknown [$6-8]

CAPITOL - WASHINGTON, D.C.

WASHINGTON, D.C. This bust of Lincoln, carved by Gutzon Borghum, was placed on display in the Capitol rotunda in 1908.
c.1918, B.S. Reynolds Co., Washington, D.C. [$2-4]

ABRAHAM LINCOLN, CAPITOL ROTUNDA, WASHINGTON, D. C.

NEW LINCOLN MEMORIAL, WASHINGTON, D. C.

26298

WASHINGTON, D.C. Construction of the $3 million Lincoln Memorial began on February 12, 1914. Designed by architect Henry Bacon, it was built in the classical style of a Greek temple. There are 36 massive columns, each representing a state in the Union at the time of Lincoln's death. The building measures 204 feet in length by 134 feet in width and is 99 feet high. Dedication ceremonies for this national landmark were held on Memorial Day, May 30, 1922. Included among the 50,000 people present was 78 year old Robert Todd Lincoln, the only surviving son of the man being honored.
c. 1920s, B.S. Reynolds Co., Washington, D.C. [$1-3]

Interior of Lincoln Memorial, Washington, D. C.

WASHINGTON, D.C. Within the memorial sits the magnificent seated likeness of Abraham Lincoln. Carved into the walls of chambers on either side of the statue are the words to his Second Inaugural and Gettysburg Address. Over one million visitors a year visit this shrine to our 16th president.
c. 1920s, B.S. Reynolds Co., Washington, D.C. [$2-4]

INTERIOR OF LINCOLN MEMORIAL, WASHINGTON, D. C.

IN THIS TEMPLE
AS IN THE HEARTS OF THE PEOPLE
FOR WHOM HE SAVED THE UNION
THE MEMORY OF ABRAHAM LINCOLN
IS ENSHRINED FOREVER

WASHINGTON, D.C. Perhaps the best known of all Lincoln statues, this masterpiece was created by the great American sculptor Daniel Chester French. Taking four years to carve, it stands 19 feet tall and is made of 175 tons of white marble from the state of Georgia. Special lighting is directed onto the statue to further enhance its awe inspiring qualities.
c. 1925, Washington News Co., Washington, D.C. [$3-5]

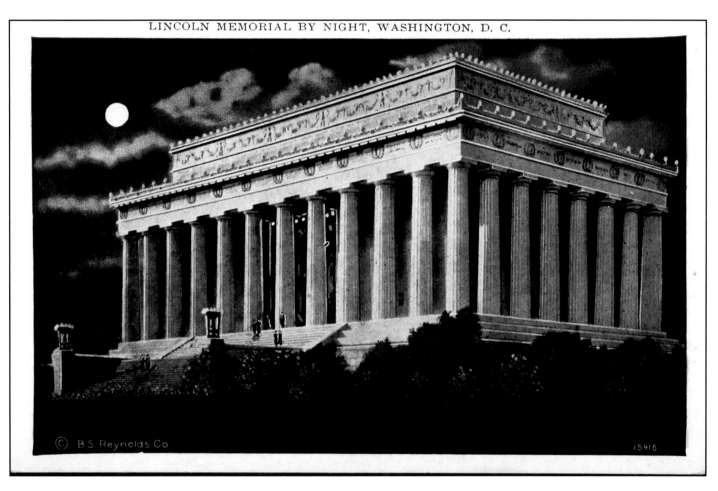

WASHINGTON, D.C. Both day and night the Lincoln memorial serves as a symbol of hope and freedom for all mankind. It is also a reminder of the great man and the sacrifices he and so many others made to insure the well being of our nation. As the inscription within the memorial states, "In this temple, as in the hearts of the people for whom he saved the Union, the memory of Abraham Lincoln is enshrined forever."
c. 1920s, B.S. Reynolds Co., Washington, D.C. [$2-4]

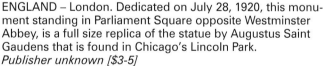

ENGLAND – London. Dedicated on July 28, 1920, this monument standing in Parliament Square opposite Westminster Abbey, is a full size replica of the statue by Augustus Saint Gaudens that is found in Chicago's Lincoln Park.
Publisher unknown [$3-5]

ENGLAND – Manchester. Referred to negatively as the "stomach ache statue" by Robert Lincoln, this memorial was originally meant for London. A replica of this work, completed by George Barnard in 1917, can be found in Cincinnati, Ohio.
c. 1930s, Publisher unknown [$4-6]

Monuments and memorials to Abraham Lincoln are not limited to the United States, but can also be found in a number of other countries. Here are several that honor this extraordinary American.

MEXICO – Ciudad Juarez. This 13 foot high statue, a gift to Ciudad Juarez from the United States, was dedicated by President Lyndon B. Johnson in 1966. In exchange, a statue of the Mexican hero Benito Juarez was placed in Washington, D.C.
c. 1960s, Roberto Studio, Ciudad Juarez, Mexico [$2-4]

SCOTLAND – Edinburgh. Unveiled on August 21, 1893 this 16 foot tall statue honors not only Abraham Lincoln but also all of the Scots who fought for the Union during the Civil War. The American artist George G. Bissell was the sculptor.
c. 1906, Ingle, Edinburgh, Scotland [$5-7]

Bibliography

Basler, Roy P., editor. *Lincoln – Speeches and Writings, 2 Vols.* New York, New York: The Library of America, 1989.

Catton, Bruce. *The American Heritage New History of the Civil War*. New York, New York: Penguin Group, 1996.

Donald, David Herbert. *Lincoln*. New York, New York: Simon & Schuster, 1995.

Kunhardt, Dorothy Meserve and Philip B. Kunhardt Jr. *Twenty Days*. New York, New York: Harper & Row, 1965.

Kunhardt, Philip B., Jr., Philip B. Kunhardt III and Peter W. Kunhardt. *Lincoln – An Illustrated Biography*. New York, New York: Alfred A. Knopf, 1992.

Lorant, Stefan. *The Life of Abraham Lincoln*. New York, New York: The New American Library, 1963.

Lorant, Stefan. *Lincoln – A Picture Story of His Life*. New York, New York: Bonanza Books, 1975.

Lowe, James L. *Lincoln Postcard Catalog*. Norwood, Pennsylvania: Deltiologists of America, 1973.

Miers, Earl S. editor in chief. *Lincoln Day by Day – A Chronology 1809-1865.* Dayton, Ohio: Morningside, 1991.

Ostendorf, Lloyd. *Lincoln's Photographs a Complete Album*. Dayton, Ohio: Rockywood Press, 1998.

Pratt, Harry E. *Abraham Lincoln Chronology*. Springfield, Illinois: Illinois State Historical Library, 1957.

Sandburg, Carl. *Abraham Lincoln the Prairie Years*. New York, New York: Harcourt, Brace and Co., 1926.

Steers, Edward, Jr., *Lincoln – A Pictorial History*. Gettysburg, Pennsylvania: Thomas Publications, 1993.

Sullivan, George. *In Their Own Words : Abraham Lincoln*. New York, New York: Scholastic Inc., 2000.

Thomas, Benjamin P. *Abraham Lincoln a Biography*. New York, New York: Barnes and Noble, 1994.